BEYOND
Salvation
THE ART OF
RECEIVING GOD'S PROMISES

Katherine Is. Free

authorHOUSE®

AuthorHouse™
1663 Liberty Drive
Bloomington, IN 47403
www.authorhouse.com
Phone: 1 (800) 839-8640

Published by AuthorHouse   03/03/2016

ISBN: 978-1-5049-7508-7 (sc)
ISBN: 978-1-5049-7509-4 (e)

Library of Congress Control Number: 2016901127

Print information available on the last page.

Any people depicted in stock imagery provided by Thinkstock are models, and such images are being used for illustrative purposes only. Certain stock imagery © Thinkstock.

This book is printed on acid-free paper.

To my Heavenly Father:
Be Thou magnified, for You have pleasure in
the prosperity of Your children!

Acknowledgments

Thank you to Chris Zafiriou, who sowed the title of his would-be book, *Beyond Salvation*.

A special thank you and God bless you to all of my spiritual mentors who have sown the Word into my life through their words, their teaching, and their example. God bless you abundantly...

Contents

Introduction

To Whom It May Concern:

Thank you for joining me on this glorious journey into the simpler, yet deeper, things of God. I will be sharing some thirst-quenching revelations that God has given me concerning His heart, His character, and His desire for mankind. As you open your heart and mind to receive—whether you are a Christian or not—I believe God will meet you right where you are and tell you everything you want to know.

I will be sharing some revelations that will challenge some of you to go deeper than you have ever gone into the things of God, as these revelations may challenge things that you have been taught and believed about God. Others of you will be reminded of things that you have learned along the way, in which case, I, like Peter, "will not be negligent to put you always in remembrance of these things, though ye know them …" (2 Peter 1:12 KJV). And still others of you will be in just the right place to receive this thirst-quenching Word for all It is worth, receiving revelations that will unlock areas in your life and usher you into a realm of freedom that you have never known.

Do you, or does anybody you know, think you're experiencing as much of God as there is to experience?

Perhaps you

- think your Christian life should be more victorious than it is;
- want to experience greater manifestation of healing, provision, and prosperity in your life;
- want to know everything that belongs to you as a child of God; or
- want to know how to access everything that belongs to you as a child of God.

Or maybe you

- know there's got to be more to life than what you are living,
- want to understand God better,
- think you have to be a "good Christian" to get to Heaven, or
- feel all churched out.

Do you

- think God is some big, impersonal, out-there God;
- think serving God is too hard and no fun; or
- think you have to give up too much to serve God?

If any of the above applies to you or anybody you know, *this concerns you.*

Whoever you are, and to whichever group you belong, I am very excited to share with you the revelations that God has shared with me. Get ready to renew your mind and to enlarge your capacity to receive. Set yourself to be in agreement with God's Word even if your mind does not yet comprehend it. By being in agreement with God's Word, you position yourself to receive wisdom, knowledge, and revelation from God that supersede your mental capacity. I invite you, according to Isaiah 54:2, to "enlarge the place of your tent ... stretch forth the curtains of thine habitations: spare not, lengthen thy cords, and strengthen thy stakes" (KJV). Let God minister directly to your inner being—to your very spirit. My prayer for all of you reading this book is that your ears be open to hear and your hearts be open to understand the Word of the Lord. I pray that you receive the Word of God that you hear through this book—not as one more human opinion, but as it is in truth, God's Word to you.[1]

God's Word is inexhaustible. There is no end to the revelation that comes through His Word. With that in mind, this book is designed to be

---

[1]   See 1 Thessalonians 2:13.

as light a read or as deep a study as you want it to be. Within the text, you will find scriptures that I have written in their entirety as well as scriptures that I have only referenced and listed in the footnotes. My prayer is that you will not be satisfied with just reading the scriptures as written in this book. Rather, my desire is that you will develop a deeper hunger for God and for His Word—a hunger that leads you to examine the scriptures for yourself and to follow where they lead.

***

Father,

Thank you for these precious ones. Give them the spirit of revelation and wisdom in the knowledge of Your Son, Jesus Christ.[2] Make them intelligent and discerning in knowing Him personally - their eyes focused and clear so they can see exactly what it is You are calling them to.[3] I speak that their appetite for You increases and that they hunger for You as never before. Thank You, Father, for satisfying the hungry soul.[4]

Holy Spirit, breathe on this Word, making it come alive to every person who reads it. I speak that souls are saved, minds are renewed, and lives are changed. I thank You, Lord, that the Word they receive works effectually in them who believe.[5] I celebrate them as they grow in the knowledge of You, and declare that they walk worthy of You, enjoying *every* Kingdom benefit to the fullest in Jesus' Name. Amen.

Love,
Katherine

---

[2]   See Ephesians 1:17.

[3]   See Ephesians 1:18 MSG.

[4]   See Psalm 107:9.

[5]   See 1 Thessalonians 2:13.

This Book Is For ...

Saved people, unsaved people, believers, and unbelievers alike—this book was written with you in mind. However, there *is* one group of people this book was *not* written for: *dis*believers. You may be asking, "What is the difference between unbelievers and disbelievers?" Allow me to explain.

Unbelievers vs. Disbelievers

Before we can distinguish an unbeliever from a disbeliever, we must first know what a believer is. According to *Webster's 1828 Dictionary*, a believer is one who believes—one who gives credit to evidence other than that of personal knowledge. When pertaining to theology, a believer is one who gives credit to the truth of the scriptures—one who receives the scriptures as not just words on a page but as revelation from God.[6] For the sake of this conversation, unbelievers are people who do not receive the scriptures as truth. Rather, they read the scriptures simply as words on a page—almost as if they were part of an ordinary story or a piece of literature. Unbelievers are not opposed to believing; they simply withhold their belief but could be persuaded to believe. Disbelievers, on the other hand, are those who flat out refuse to believe the scriptures are true because they have consciously chosen not to do so. No amount of reasoning or persuasion can get them to change their mind. They simply refuse to believe.

We see a picture of believers and disbelievers side by side in the book of Hebrews. In Hebrews chapter 3, the author recalls how the children of Israel provoked God in the wilderness with their unbelief. After seeing His wondrous works and hearing His commandments and statutes for forty years, they still did not believe.

---

[6]   *An American Dictionary of the English Language*, 1ˢᵗ edition, (hereafter cited as "Webster").

> For some, when they had heard, did provoke [God] …
> And to whom sware He that they should not enter into His rest,
> but to them that believed not?
> So we see that they could not enter in *because of unbelief*" (Hebrews
> 3:16, 18–19, emphasis added).

The Amplified Bible translation (Classic Edition) of verse 19 says, "unbelief had shut them out." (In Greek—the original language of the New Testament—the word translated as "unbelief" means "disbelief" or "lack of Christian faith."[7] It is derived from the Greek word that is used to describe people who reject or refuse God's in-birthing of faith.[8]) The author goes on to say in Hebrews 4:2:

> For indeed we have had the glad tidings [Gospel of God] proclaimed to us just as truly as they [the Israelites of old did when the good news of deliverance from bondage came to them]; *but the message they heard did not benefit them, because it was not mixed with faith* (with the leaning of the entire personality on God in absolute trust and confidence in His power, wisdom, and goodness) *by those who heard it; neither were they united in faith with the ones* [Joshua and Caleb] *who heard (did believe)*" (Amplified, Classic Edition, emphasis added).

The "we" in this scripture refers to New Testament saints, or people who became Christians after Jesus ascended to Heaven, who heard the gospel and believed it. The "they" refers to the children of Israel in Moses' day, when God sent Moses to tell Pharaoh to let His people go so they could worship Him. The children of Israel, all except for Joshua and

---

7   J. Strong, W. Baker, and S. Zodhiates, *AMG's Annotated Strong's Greek Dictionary of the New Testament*, (Chattanooga, Tennessee: AMG, 1992) (hereafter cited as *Strong's Greek*), word 570.

8   Ibid., word 571.

Caleb—despite the many displays of God's power, wisdom, and goodness toward them – still did not believe God when He said He would lead them to the Promised Land. God had sent them out of Egypt with riches; parted the Red Sea, granting them safe passage on dry land; defeated their enemies before their very eyes; sweetened bitter water; and provided food from Heaven. Yet they still *chose* not to believe.[9]

At God's command, Moses sent ten men to spy out the land. Eight men returned with an evil report, or a report of unbelief:[10] *The inhabitants are too strong, giants live there, the cities are fortified, we are like grasshoppers compared to them* … Only two spies returned with a good report: *We are well able, they are bread for us, their defense is departed from them, and the Lord is with us!*

The people chose to believe the evil report of unbelief; they chose not to believe that God would give them the land He had promised them. Thus, they were incapable of receiving His promise. Joshua and Caleb— the two men that came back with the good report—were the only two from that generation who believed God. Thus they were the only two from that generation who were able to receive God's promise of entering the Promised Land.[11]

So we see that Joshua and Caleb were believers, while the other Israelites in their generation were disbelievers. Despite infallible proofs, they deliberately chose not to believe God. The same gospel can be preached to different people, but only those who mix it with faith (i.e., believe God's Word)—will benefit from it.[12] *Are you a believer?*

---

[9]   See Exodus 12:35–25; 14:10–31; 15:22–26; 16:2–15.

[10]   See Hebrews 3:12.

[11]   See Numbers 13, 14.

[12]   See Hebrews 4:2.

Unbelievers

As explained earlier, unbelievers are people who do not believe but could be persuaded to believe. Perhaps these people do not believe because they have not been presented with the proper knowledge. Perhaps they have been raised in religious tradition their entire lives and find it difficult to believe anything else. Whatever the reason, there are many unbelievers where the Word of God is concerned.

It is easy, and maybe even natural, to assume that people who are not saved—who have not accepted Jesus Christ as their Lord and Savior—are unbelievers. However, you may be surprised to know that there are many Christians who are unbelievers as well. I have heard these people referred to as unbelieving believers. Unbelieving believers are people who have received Jesus as their Savior but who do not believe that God's Word is true. *"Is this possible?"* you may ask. Why, yes, it is. Let's see what God has to say about it.

In Hosea 4:6, God says, "My people are destroyed for lack of knowledge." The *New Living Translation* reads, "My people are being destroyed because they don't know Me." *The Message* translation reads, "My people are ruined because they don't know what's right or true." Notice that in each translation, God says, "My people." He is not referring to the world (i.e., unsaved people). No, He is referring to His chosen people—Israel during the Old Testament days, and the body of Christ in the present day. Thus we see that it is possible for people to be Christians but still not know God or His Truth, Who is Jesus.

In the mouth of two or three witnesses shall every word be established.[13] Before calling my witnesses, let me offer a bit of a disclaimer: In the two accounts I am about to share, the people are not technically Christians, because when they were called, Jesus had not yet been crucified

---

[13] See 2 Corinthians 13:1.

or raised from the dead. However, they were God's chosen, and their accounts are sufficient for the present discussion.

Our first witness comes from the Old Testament in 1 Kings 18:21. The prophet Elijah asked God's chosen people, the children of Israel, how long they would falter between two opinions. He said, "If the LORD be God, follow Him: but if Baal, then follow him." The Israelites had no idea who the true God was, for the scripture goes on to say, "And the people answered him not a word." They did not know who to follow because they did not know who God was. However, when the Israelites saw the awesome display of God's power, "they fell on their faces: and they said, 'The LORD, He is the God: the LORD, He is the God'" (1 Kings 18:39). Once presented with the truth of who God was, they became believers.

Our second witness comes from the New Testament. In Mark chapter 16 we see that after three years of walking with Jesus, witnessing the miracles of Jesus, and even ministering with the power and authority Jesus had given them, the disciples did not believe the Word that Jesus had spoken to them concerning His death and resurrection.[14] Jesus had explained to them that He would go to Jerusalem; suffer ill treatment by the elders, chief priests, and scribes; be killed; and then be raised on the third day.[15] Yet we see in Mark 16 that when the disciples received report that Jesus was alive, they did not believe it:

> After Jesus rose from the dead early on Sunday morning, the first person who saw Him was Mary Magdalene, the woman from whom He had cast out seven demons.
>
> She went to THE DISCIPLES, who were grieving and weeping, and told them what had happened.
>
> But when she told them that Jesus was alive and she had seen Him, THEY DIDN'T BELIEVE HER.

---

[14] See Luke 9:1–6.

[15] See Matthew 16:21, Mark 9:31.

Afterward He appeared in a different form to two of His followers who were walking from Jerusalem into the country.

They rushed back to tell the others, BUT NO ONE BELIEVED THEM.

Still later He appeared to the eleven disciples as they were eating together. He *rebuked* them for their *stubborn unbelief* because THEY REFUSED TO BELIEVE THOSE WHO HAD SEEN HIM AFTER HE HAD BEEN RAISED FROM THE DEAD (Mark 16:9–14 NLT, emphasis added).

Jesus' own disciples did not believe that He had risen from the dead. They did not believe that Jesus had done what He said He would do—even after others told them that He had done it! This unbelief is an indication of their not knowing the truth of who Jesus was. Though they had kept company with Him, they still did not know Him. However, once Jesus revealed His resurrected Self to them, none of them dared to ask who He was, because they *knew* He was the Lord.[16] Like the children of Israel in 1 Kings, once presented with the truth of who Jesus was, the disciples became believers.

Are you a believer? What will it take for you to become one? For the children of Israel in the above account, it took an introduction by way of the manifestation of God's power. For the disciples, it took Jesus presenting Himself to them personally. Perhaps, like the children of Israel, you have no idea who God is or what sets Him apart from other gods. Or maybe, like the disciples, you have kept company with God—praying, attending church services, and even working in the ministry—but you still do not have a personal knowledge of who He is or how He feels about you. The purpose of this book is to share the love of God with you – enlightening you to His heart and His character, to usher you into (deeper) relationship with Him, and to enlighten you to all of your Kingdom benefits as a child of such a loving God.

---

[16]   See John 20:19, 24–28; 21:1–14.

Whether you are curious about the Christian walk, just beginning the Christian journey, or have been on this journey for a while, my desire is to set you up for God to make a believer out of you. I am so excited that God has brought you to this place, and I am even more excited about the place He is taking you to. I join the Apostle Paul in asking God to strengthen you by His Spirit—not with a brute strength, but with a glorious inner strength—that Christ will live in you as you open the door and invite Him in. And I ask Him that with both feet planted firmly on love, you'll be able to take in with all Christians the extravagant dimensions of Christ's love. Reach out and experience the breadth! Test its length! Plumb the depths! Rise to the heights! Live full lives, full in the fullness of God.[17]

It is now my privilege and my honor to introduce to some and present to others the

> ever-loving,
>> ever-faithful,
>>> ever-cheerful
>>>> Giver
>>>>> of every good
>>>>>> and
>>>>>>> every perfect
>>>>>>>> gift!

---

[17] See Ephesians 3:16–19 MSG.

Open Invitation

Before we begin, I just want to extend this invitation to you: If at any point while reading this book you decide that you want to receive Jesus Christ as your Savior and Lord, you are more than welcome to do so. You do not have to wait until you finish reading the book, or until you go to church, or until … whenever. You can receive Him the very moment you decide. Simply believe that Jesus is the Son of the living God and that He died on the cross and rose again to make all of God's promises available to you. As soon as you receive Him *for Who He is,* all that He died and rose again to give you is yours. All that is left for you to do is receive!

If you would like to receive Jesus as your Savior and make Him your Lord, please allow me the privilege of leading you in the following prayer. Pray these words aloud:

Jesus,

I receive You as my Savior, and I make you my Lord. I believe that You are the Son of God and that You died and rose again just for me. You died. You rose. And now You are seated at the right hand of God. I believe that You bore my sin and took my judgment so I would not have to. I believe You took sickness and disease so I would not have to. I believe You took poverty and lack so I would not have to. I believe that You did it all for me. You gave Your life for me. I renounce my past. I renounce the devil and everything he stands for. I turn to You. Take my life and do something wonderful with it. Thank You, Jesus.

Hallelujah!

Welcome to the Family!

If you prayed that prayer in sincerity, you are born again! You are a child of God! Now that you have received Jesus, God's Holy Spirit lives inside of you. But this is just the beginning!

There is new power available to you to learn and to maintain all that you have just received. It is by and through this power that you will be able to live out all that God has given you. He has made this power available to you through the baptism of His precious Holy Spirit *if* you would like to receive it. He will not force you to receive it. Though the Holy Spirit lives inside You, He will not just overtake you. You must *receive* the baptism of the Holy Spirit just as you *received* salvation through Jesus. To learn more about the Holy Spirit and the power that the baptism of the Holy Spirit affords you, see Appendix C.

Ask God to lead you to a Bible-believing church where you will be taught the Word of God without compromise, where you can grow in the Lord and in the things of God. Welcome to the family!

Part I

Salvation vs. Religion

Religion has painted the picture of people having to follow a bunch of rules and go through a bunch of changes to "get right" before they can experience the goodness of the Lord. This inaccurate portrayal has resulted in people trying to achieve salvation in their own strength, not even understanding what salvation is. They think salvation is about acting right or being a good person. Therefore, they become discouraged when they fall short, and they begin to doubt their salvation.

Salvation is not about acting right but about being made right. Second Corinthians 5:21 tells us that He who knew no sin became sin that we might be made the righteousness of God. The only thing we can do to become righteous is believe on Jesus—the One who makes us righteous. Once we believe that we have *been made* righteous and *receive* our righteousness, the pressure is off us to *become* righteous. We will begin to behave righteously because it is right believing that leads to right living.[18] Getting saved is not nearly as complicated or burdensome as religion has made it out to be. It's not even about "getting saved" as much as it is about *receiving* salvation.

Don't get me wrong. We *do* "get saved." I remember going outside to play with my friends when I was eight years old. When I got outside, everyone was so excited. They couldn't wait to tell me, "Mrs. H. got saved! Mrs. H. got saved!" I had no idea what they were talking about.

---

[18]   Joseph Prince, pastor of New Creation Church in Singapore, coined the phrase "Right believing leads to right living." I highly recommend his teaching *Right Believing Leads to Right Living*, available on his website at www.josephprince.org.

"Saved from what?" I asked. I didn't know what she had been saved from, but I knew that I wanted to be saved too. I didn't want anything bad to get me.

For those of you wondering as I did, I am delighted to tell you that we get saved from death, or eternal separation from God.[19] We get saved from condemnation[20] and eternal punishment in Hell.[21] We get saved from the dominion of sin.[22] The devil no longer has reign over us! However, if we look at the salvation experience only through the lens of "getting saved," there is the potential to miss out on experiencing salvation itself.

Salvation is about relationship, not about religion. When we enter into relationship with Jesus, we *receive* His love. We *receive* His provision. We *receive* His guidance. We *receive* the victory that results from *receiving* His love, provision, and guidance, which equip us to overcome battles and shortcomings. In religion, people often *fear* that God will reject them: they *fear* that God will be angry at them or *fear* that God will abandon them. They rarely experience victory because they have an inaccurate perception of who God is. In trying to "be right with God," they do not realize that through Jesus they are already *made* right *in* God. This is one reason so many Christians live beneath their Kingdom benefits. If Christians would just learn to *receive*!

When we receive salvation, we are born again. We are a new creature.[23] As far as this earthly realm is concerned, we have died; our new, real life is hidden with Christ in God.[24] Many zealous and well-meaning Christians become frustrated and get burned out trying to achieve in their own strength what Jesus has already provided for them through grace.

---

[19]   See Romans 6:23.

[20]   See John 3:18, Romans 8:1.

[21]   See Matthew 25:46.

[22]   See Romans 6:6–7.

[23]   See 2 Corinthians 5:17.

[24]   See Colossians 3:3 AB.

Grace is God's undeserved favor. There is no way to earn it. If you could earn it, it wouldn't be grace. If you could pay it back, it wouldn't be grace. If you could make it up to God, it wouldn't be grace. The only proper thing you can do with God's grace is *receive* it. So many people are in a fear-based relationship with God born out of the rules and regulations of religion rather than in a love-based relationship born out of the free gift of grace. They do not recognize God for the loving God that He is.

Isn't it amazing how two people can be in the same relationship but view the relationship through totally different lenses? I was engaged to a gentleman once. I was completely in love with him and shared my whole world with him. As far as I was concerned, everything I had was his—even my time.

I was always available when he called (we were in a long-distance relationship, and lived in different time zones). If he needed anything and I had it, it was his. If there was anything he wanted and I knew about it (well – *almost* anything), it was his—many times before he would even ask. I knew what kind of food he liked, what his favorite colors were, his favorite TV shows and pastimes, and even who his favorite authors were. When I knew he was coming to town, I arranged my schedule to pick him up at the airport, spend time with him, and take him to his family's home. If possible, I would arrange my work schedule so he could have my car during the day.

I made sure the refrigerator and cabinets were stocked with his favorite snacks so when he came over, he would have plenty that he liked to eat. I planned outings to go see his favorite performers. I wore his favorite color… you get the picture. I enjoyed every moment that we spent together—even when the moments were not so pleasant. I was always excited to hear from him, even more excited to see him. NEVER liked saying good-bye to him—not even when I knew I would see him in a few minutes.

I know. I sound like a lovesick puppy. But I loved him. I understand Mariah Carey when she sings, "Far too much is never enough."[25] However, the day came when my fiancé told me he was leaving. He told me he was not ready to get married. Of course I was sad. I was hurt. I felt disillusioned. (But I understood that I had a part to play in that—a big part.) The day that we parted, the only words I had for him were words of love. Not an evil, mean, or angry word. Just love, love, well wishes, and more love.

His words for me were words of love as well. We continued to talk over the phone for a couple of weeks after we parted. I was taken aback when he said to me, "You know, it would be really easy for us to be angry at each other. But we're not. I'm really proud of us for that." I had no idea what he was talking about. To this day, I still don't know. Though he had left two days before we were to be married, I did not have one ill thought or feeling about him. I just loved him.

Don't get too angry, ladies! Leaving me then was the noblest thing he could have ever done for me. He could have left me at the altar, after our first child was born, or after twenty years of marriage. He did right by me, and I love him for it!

When he said it would be easy for us to be angry at each other, I remember thinking (and still think) that we must have been in two different relationships. I had nothing against him and – even though there were plenty of opportunities to be angry about things that transpired during the relationship and the present ordeal was quite painful –I could not think of anything to be angry with him about.

Evidently, he felt differently. Imagine how surprised I was when he told me he was afraid of me. (He did not explain why. In fact, he said he didn't know why.) My head went *tilt, tilt, tilt. Does – not- compute.* Fear and love cannot occupy the same space. Reflecting on various conversations that we had over the course of our relationship, it is my heartfelt belief that

---

[25] Mariah Carey, "Joy Ride," from *The Emancipation of Mimi*, Island Records, B0007GAERG, 2005.

he wore himself out trying to "be worthy" of my love, so to speak, instead of just receiving it.

I wonder if God looks at us sometimes and thinks that He and some of His children are in two different relationships: He is lavishing His love upon them, and they are walking around afraid of Him—maybe because they feel unworthy within themselves or maybe even because they think He is angry with them. Sadly, just as my fiancé did not view me the same way I viewed him, many of God's children do not view Him the same way He views them.

God views us through the lens of love: Love that covers a multitude of sin.[26] Love that pays no attention to a suffered wrong. Love that bears up under anything and everything that comes. Love that is ready to believe the best of every person. Love whose hopes are fadeless under all circumstances. Love that endures everything without weakening. Love that never fails. Love that never fades out or becomes obsolete or comes to an end.[27]

God *loves* us! There is nothing we can do to earn His love. There is nothing we can do to make Him love us more, and there is nothing we can do to make Him love us less. *God simply loves us.* He has loved us since before the foundation of the world. He demonstrates His love for us in that He spared not His own Son.[28] Rather, He gave His all and He gave His best. While we were *still* sinners—before we were even thinking about Him—His Son, Jesus Christ, died for us.[29] God did not wait for us to become worthy or to earn His love. We wouldn't be able to anyway! He didn't even wait to see if we would return His love. He loved us simply because He *is* Love.

26　See 1 Peter 4:8.

27　See 1 Corinthians 13:7-8a Amplified Bible, Classic Edition

28　See Romans 8:32.

29　See Romans 5:8.

Where salvation is concerned, it is not something that we have to worry ourselves with qualifying for. On the contrary, it is something that God absolutely wants to give us! He wants us to have it more than we want to have it! He wants us to come to Heaven more than we want to go! He wants us healed more than we want to be healed! He wants us prosperous more than we want to be prosperous! Do you see a trend here? But God is a gentleman. He will not force Himself upon us. He loves us so much that He will give us every opportunity to receive His Son, but He will also reserve our right to go to Hell if that is what we choose.

Why Do People Go to Hell?

Despite what religion has taught, there is only one sin for which people go to hell: that of *not believing on Jesus*.[30,31] I know. I know. This is a strong statement, and it contradicts what many of you have always believed. Remember—set yourself to be in agreement with God's Word even if your mind does not yet comprehend it. If you are open to receiving the truth,

---

[30] See John 16:9.

[31] Many object to this assertion, saying that the one unpardonable sin is the blasphemy of the Holy Ghost (Mark 3:29). While this objection is not incorrect, it is incomplete. Blasphemy against the Holy Ghost occurs when one has "tasted of the heavenly gift, …[was] made [a partaker] of the Holy Ghost, …[has] tasted the good Word of God and the powers of the world to come" (Hebrews 6:4-5), and then decides to turn away from God. Hence, blasphemy against the Holy Ghost can only be committed by one who has walked in seasoned, mature relationship with Christ. According to Hebrews 6:4, 6, it is impossible for those who were once enlightened to the gospel of Jesus Christ to be renewed again unto repentance, "seeing they crucify to themselves the Son of God afresh, and put Him to an open shame." In other words, they have chosen not to believe on Jesus. Thus, not believing on Jesus and blaspheming the Holy Ghost are two sides of the same coin.

the truth is what you will receive. That being said, let me share a story with you, and then we will go straight to the Word of God.

It was not long after I began writing this section of the book that I met a young man. My assistant and I had gone shopping to pick up some supplies and were leaving the store. As soon as we stepped out of the door, a young man approached us, wanting us to purchase his CD. He was a young, aspiring rap artist—nineteen years old. I looked at his CD and asked him what his message was. He told me the CD was about how he had overcome trials and tribulations, and he assured me that the music contained no profanity. I told him that I would purchase his CD, but that I wanted to share something with him first. He agreed to listen. I asked him if he was familiar with the concept of sowing and reaping. He said he was. I then explained to him that I was sowing to support him in his musical endeavors, believing that I would reap a harvest of supporters for my literary endeavors, as I was in the process of writing a book (this book). Before I could ask him more about his CD, he asked me about my book.

This is the first time I had been asked to explain the contents of this book to someone I did not know. Not knowing where to start, I said, "It's about salvation. Do you know Jesus?" He said he did. So I began to explain very generally how religion has presented Christians with a lot of misinformation, which has led to their having inaccurate perceptions of God and salvation. I went on to explain that God is a God of love; He is not some out-there-somewhere God who does not care about us or who is angry with us, just waiting to punish us every chance He gets. Rather, I explained, He is a loving God, and He loves us so much that He gave His Son Jesus so we could live the wonderful life that He had planned for us from before the foundation of the world.

I had found a rhythm in describing the book by then, and I began to explain that the only sin people go to hell for is the sin of not believing in Jesus—that it is not their sinful acts that send them to hell.

My rhythm was suddenly interrupted when the young man said, "Sista, Sista, Sista, Sista! Wait a minute. I have to stop you right there." I listened as he began to almost scold me for telling people such a thing. His first objection was that God is not all love, but that God is a man of war.[32] I did not debate him. Rather, I imparted to him the knowledge that he was missing.

"Yes, God is a man of war," I said. "Tell me someone you love."

"My little brother."

"If someone were to try to harm your little brother, would you just stand there and let it happen, or would you do everything in your power to protect him?"

Almost indignantly, he said, "I would protect him!"

"Exactly, man of war! You love your little brother and if anyone messes with him, they've got to deal with you. It's the same way with God. If anyone messes with His children, they've got to deal with Him. God doesn't play about His children."

He went on to say, "But at the same time, if my little brother does wrong, I have to punish him."

"Yes," I agreed, "just like God chastises those whom He loves."[33] He was beginning to understand but still was not without objection.

He told me that people must obey God's laws, precepts, and commands to go to Heaven. I maintained that people must receive Jesus as their Savior and Lord to go to Heaven, and I then expounded that if people

---

[32] See Exodus 15:3.

[33] See Hebrews 12:6; Proverbs 3:12. The word translated "chasteneth" in Hebrews 12:6 means to correct (Strong's Greek, word 3811). The word translated "correcteth" in Proverbs 3:12 means to reprove of sin, and is pictured as a demonstration of love (James Strong, W. Baker, & S. Zodhiates, AMG's Annotated Strong's Hebrew Dictionary of the Old Testament, (hereafter cited as *Strong's Hebrew*) (Chattanooga, Tennessee: AMG, 1992.), word 3198).

truly receive Jesus as their Savior and Lord, they will obey God's laws, precepts, and commands. He was appalled that I would say such a thing.

"You mean to tell me that serial killers and murderers can accept Jesus and keep killing people and won't go to Hell?"

"No," I assured him. "If someone says they accepted Jesus but continues to enjoy doing the sinful things they used to do, I can assure you that they did not receive Jesus. When we receive Jesus as our Lord and Savior, our very nature is changed. We are no longer sinners. It will take our minds and bodies some time to catch up, however, so yes we will continue to engage in sinful acts. But we will no longer feel comfortable doing them; we will no longer enjoy them as we once did."

He continued to refer back to the laws, precepts, and commands. He said, "People keep saying that the law is done away with, but if it wasn't for the law, I wouldn't know I was sinning."[34]

"I never said that the law was done away with," I assured him.[35] (People need the law so they will recognize their need for Jesus.) "It's just that people who have received Jesus are no longer *under the curse* of the law."[36]

I explained that God loved us so much that He made a new covenant.[37] The old covenant was between God and His people. God had to treat them according to how they behaved. If they did good, they got good. If they did bad, they got bad. But God didn't want us to get bad *at all.*[38] So He made a new covenant—*with Himself!* In this covenant, He is no longer bound to give us bad when we do bad or to give us good only when we do good. He can give us good *even* when we do bad. (It is called God's grace – His undeserved favor.) Even when we are faithless, He is

---

[34]   See 1 Corinthians 15:6.

[35]   See Matthew 5:17.

[36]   See Galatians 3:13.

[37]   See Jeremiah 31:31; Hebrews 8:8, 13.

[38]   See Hebrews 8:12.

faithful.[39] He said He would write His laws in our hearts and in our minds so we wouldn't need anyone to teach us. He would be our God, and we would be His people.[40]

The young man argued that God wrote His laws only in the hearts and minds of prophets. "What about Pentecost?" I asked.

"I don't know nothin' about Pentecost." As far as he was concerned, Pentecost didn't have anything to do with anything.

In the New Testament, Pentecost is when God poured His Holy Spirit out upon all flesh.[41] When we receive Jesus, the Holy Spirit comes to live on the inside of us.[42] He teaches us how to live the Christian life. He guides us and directs us.[43] He reminds us that we are the righteousness of God; when we sin, He reminds us who we are in Christ Jesus and helps us to overcome that area of sin in our lives.

My assistant had been watching this whole exchange. She finally joined the conversation. She said, "I am only watching from the side, but you two are saying the same thing. You're just saying it in your nineteen-year-old version, and she is saying it in her her-age version: God is a holy God, and only the righteous can go to Heaven. Isn't that what you're saying?"

"Yes."

When my assistant said that he was saying it in his nineteen-year-old version and I was saying it in my my-age version, she was discerning that we were each speaking according to our level of understanding. She captured the very essence of what I explained in the beginning of this book: "My people perish for lack of knowledge" (God speaking). It is obvious that this young man loved God. He was just lacking knowledge.

---

39   See 2 Timothy 2:13.

40   See Jeremiah 31:33–34; Hebrews 8:10.

41   See Acts 2:1–19.

42   See 1 Corinthians 3:16; 1 Corinthians 6:19; Galatians 4:6.

43   See John 16:13.

(He reminds me of Saul of Tarsus before he became the Apostle Paul. He had a zeal for God, but that zeal was not according to the knowledge of God.[44])

This young man was very passionate, full of conviction, and not afraid to stand up for his God. So much so that when I started to give him the money for his CD partway through our conversation, he told me to keep my money and to give him his CD back, quoting 1 Corinthians 6:14, which says to be not unequally yoked with unbelievers.

Come to find out, he was a Hebrew Israelite.[45] But he was open to hearing truth.

To God be the glory for the seeds that were planted and watered and that will continue to be watered. I believe God that this young man will come to the saving knowledge of Jesus Christ and that he will receive the baptism of the Holy Ghost. I declare that he will be a light and a witness among his Hebrew Israelite brothers and sisters, bringing them to the saving knowledge of Jesus Christ, in Jesus' Name.

I shared this story to acknowledge that I realize this truth I am about to share about why people go to Hell ruffles feathers more than just a little bit. This gentleman was a Hebrew Israelite, but I have encountered many people from other religions—including Christianity—who find it difficult to embrace this teaching as well. Nonetheless, in the mouths of two or three witnesses shall every word be established.[46] Both of the witnesses I will call upon come from the New Testament.

In John 16:8–9, Jesus, speaking of the Holy Spirit, explains, "And when He is come, He will reprove the world of sin, and of righteousness, and of judgment: OF SIN, BECAUSE THEY BELIEVE NOT ON ME"

---

[44] See Romans 10:2.

[45] For information about what Hebrew Israelites believe, see *25 Beliefs of the Hebrew Israelites—the Levites* at http://haitianisraelites.weebly.com/25-beliefs-of-the-hebrew-israelites.html.

[46] See 2 Corinthians 13:1.

(KJV, emphasis added). The Amplified Bible (Classic Edition) says, "About sin, *because they do not believe in Me [Trust in, rely on, and adhere to Me]*" (emphasis added). *The Message* translation says, "He'll show them that *their refusal to believe Me is their basic sin*" (emphasis added).

My second witness can be found in Romans 6:23, where we learn that "the wages of sin is death but the gift of God is eternal life *through Jesus Christ*, our Lord" (emphasis added). People do not go to hell because of their sins (plural), but for the singular sin of not believing on Jesus. Ask yourself, if people did go to hell because of sinful acts they committed, which sin would be the one that sends them to hell? Which sin could they stop doing that would allow them to go to heaven?

Am I telling you that you can believe on Jesus and continue engaging in your sinful acts as usual? No, Beloved. As I explained to the nineteen-year-old over a year ago, if you believe on Jesus and continue to enjoy engaging in your sinful acts, you did not really believe on Him to begin with. From the very moment you believe on Jesus and receive Him as your Savior, you are a new creature. "… If any man be in Christ, he is a new creature: old things are passed away; behold all things are become new" (2 Corinthians 5:17).

As a new creature, you will not feel comfortable doing the same things you used to do, going the same places you used to go, saying the same things you used to say, or even thinking the same thoughts you used to think. You instantly, on no part of your own (other than choosing to receive Jesus), become the righteousness of God.[47] You are not a sinner anymore. You have been saved by grace from sin's dominion over your life.[48] Your very nature (spirit) changes instantly. It just takes a while for

---

[47]   See 2 Corinthians 5:21.

[48]   See Romans 6:14.

your mind and body to catch up.[49] So though you may continue to engage in sinful acts, you will not enjoy them or feel comfortable doing them as you once did. As you grow in Jesus and in the knowledge of who He is and what He has done for you, you become more and more like Him and those sinful acts become a thing of the past. But it all starts with the simple act of believing on Jesus and receiving the free gift of salvation that He died and rose again to give you.[50]

What Is Salvation?

Over the years, religion has minimized the meaning of salvation in such a way that it only signifies a guaranteed entrance to Heaven; it provides no recourse as to how to live victoriously on earth. However, I would like for you to consider the following. Romans 10:9–10 tells us:

> "… If thou shalt confess with thy mouth the Lord Jesus, and shalt believe in thine heart that God hath raised Him from the dead, thou shalt be SAVED. For with the heart man believeth unto righteousness; and with the mouth confession is made unto SALVATION" (KJV, emphasis added).

---

[49] Man is a three-part being consisting of spirit, soul, and body. (See 2 Thessalonians 5:23.) The spirit is the real us—the part that communes with God. The soul consists of our mind, will, and emotions. The body is the part of us that enables us to interact with this earthly realm, largely led by the five senses. I highly recommend Andrew Wommack's teaching, *Spirit, Soul, and Body* to gain better understanding. It is available for download and for purchase at Andrew Wommack Ministries International (www.awmi.net).

[50] See Romans 5:12–21. Because of one man's (Adam's) sin, judgment and condemnation came upon all men. Even so, by the righteousness of one man— Jesus—the free gift of justification came upon all men.

13

The word "saved" in the original language is "*sozo*" (sode-zo), which means

- to be saved from danger;
- to be saved from suffering;
- to be saved from sickness; to be made whole
  - ○ The idea of being made whole is *shalom* in Hebrew: Nothing missing, nothing broken.[51]
- spiritual and eternal salvation;
- God's *present* power to deliver from the bondage of sin; and
- Deliverance from the wrath of God at the end of this age.[52]

The noun form of the English word "saved" is "salvation." The word "salvation" in the original language is "*soteria*" (so-tay-ree'-ah),[53] which speaks of

- deliverance, preservation, salvation;
- material and temporal deliverance from danger and apprehension (e.g., economic calamity, health issues, natural disasters, etc.);
- spiritual and eternal deliverance;
- God's present power to deliver from the bondage of sin; and
- inclusivity—to sum up *all* the blessings bestowed by God on men in Christ through the Holy Spirit.

As you can see, salvation means so much more than just guaranteed entrance to Heaven. Salvation includes *all* the blessings bestowed by God on men in Christ through the Holy Spirit—be they financial blessings, physical blessings, mental blessings, emotional blessings, vocational blessings, social blessings, or relational blessings—any kind of blessings you need! God's blessings are His promises. The Bible is *full* of them!

---

[51] *Strong's Hebrew*, word 4982.

[52] Ibid., Greek 4982.

[53] Ibid., Greek 4991.

There was a commercial years ago for Prego spaghetti sauce. In the commercial, a father playfully criticized his son, who had recently gotten married. After only 6 months of marriage, the wife had started using spaghetti sauce from a jar rather than making the sauce homemade. The father took it upon himself to give his son some marital advice by sharing with him the ingredients for a successful marriage:

"Garlic."

The son responded—speaking of the spaghetti sauce, of course— "It's in there."

"Little bits of herbs and onions for that homemade taste."

"It's in there."

Just when the father was about to make another objection, the son raised the spoon to his father's lips bidding him to taste. The son overcame his father's every objection with one response: "It's in there." And when his father still did not believe, he let him taste for himself.

Salvation is like Prego spaghetti sauce. Whatever promise you need, it's in there! Salvation is so comprehensive. I like to refer to it as the *Sozo Package!*[54] Forgiveness is part of your *Sozo Package*. Grace is part of your *Sozo Package*. The Holy Spirit is part of your *Sozo Package*. Are you ready to receive your *Sozo Package*?

"But what about asking God to forgive me for my sins?" you may ask. God has already forgiven you, my friend. Once you receive Jesus as your Savior, your sins are forgiven and God will never again be angry with you. That is not to say that He will not chastise you, for He chastises those whom He loves.[55] However, God has so completely forgiven your sins that He chooses not to remember them anymore. See for yourself:

---

[54] The *Sozo Package* consists of every blessing that being saved by grace and becoming the righteousness of God makes you eligible to receive. Kingdom benefits. See Ephesians 1:3, 2 Peter 1:3.

[55] See Proverbs 3:12; Hebrews 12:6; see footnote 32.

[God speaking through the Prophet Isaiah]: ... For as I have sworn that the waters of Noah would no longer cover the earth, so have I sworn that I would not be angry with you, nor rebuke you.[56] (Isaiah 54:9 NKJV)

For I will be merciful to their unrighteousness, and their sins and their iniquities will I remember no more. (Hebrews 8:12 KJV)
He [God] forgives all my sins and heals all my diseases. (Psalm 103:3 NLT)

He [God] has removed our sins as far from us as the east is from the west. (Psalm 103:12 NLT)

"But what about repenting?" I hear you ask. You repented when you decided to receive Jesus.

"What?!"

Yes. You repented when you received Jesus as your Savior and confessed Him as Lord; you turned away from your way of living and turned to God's way of living. Contrary to what many of us have been taught, the word "repent" does not mean "to apologize" or even "to ask forgiveness." The Greek word translated "repent" is *"metanoia,"* which means "a change of mind."[57] There is another word translated "repent" that means "to have regret, sorrow, or remorse," but this is not that word.[58]

---

56 In Isaiah 54:9, the term "rebuke" means "pour out My righteous anger on you" (see *Strong's Concordance of the Old Testament*, word 1605.). The term "rebuke" differs from the term "chastise" in that while God will never again pour out His righteous anger on His children, He *will* correct us as a demonstration of His love. (See *Strong's Dictionary of the Old Testament*, word 3198.)

57 *Strong's Greek*, word 3341.

58 Compare definitions of *"metanoia"* (3341) and *"metamellomai"* (3338) in *Strong's Greek*.

To repent in this context is to turn *from* the wrong way of doing things to God's way of doing things. It means to turn *from* our wrong way of thinking to God's right way of thinking, which will ultimately result in our turning *from* sin to righteousness.

Once you make this active decision to turn from your sin to God, *receive* God's grace to overcome this area of sin in your life. God's grace is His unmerited favor. It is, as I heard Kenneth Copeland explain, "God's desire to treat us as if sin never existed," for it is God's goodness that leads man to repentance.[59] Repentance is not a one-time thing. It is a way of life for believers, which happens only through a constant renewing of the mind through the Word of God. Renew your mind to receive the goodness of God and watch His goodness transform your life.

---

[59]   See Romans 2:4.

Part II

How Do I Receive?

Some of you may be asking, "*Why do I need to learn to receive?*" The answer is simple: because many Christians don't know how to. Think about it for a moment. How many Christians do you know—faithful and strong in the faith as they may be—that still walk around sick? Broke? In poor-quality relationships? The fact of the matter is there are many Christians who still do not understand the art of receiving God's promises. If they did, they would be living healthy, prosperous, and victorious lives.

Whether receiving salvation or the promises of God, the process is the same. We have just learned to make the process more difficult than it is. Whether you are just now joining the family, or whether you have been a Christian for years, pay close attention to this section and prepare to renew your mind. This information changed my life forever, and changes it afresh every time I meditate on it. I believe it will change your life and the lives of those around you as well. First I will discuss what it means to receive. Then I will discuss how to receive salvation, for without Jesus, none of the other promises apply. Yet with Him, every promise is yes and amen![60]

I am reminded of a story that expresses this very sentiment:

---

[60]   See 2 Corinthians 1:20.

Who Will Take the Son?[61]
author unknown

A wealthy man and his son loved to collect rare works of art. They had everything in their collection, from Picasso to Raphael. They would often sit together and admire the great works of art.

When the Viet Nam conflict broke out, the son went to war. He was very courageous and died in battle while rescuing another soldier.

The father was notified and grieved deeply for his only son.

About a month later, just before Christmas, there was a knock at the door. A young man stood at the door with a large package in his hands.

He said, "Sir, you don't know me, but I am the soldier for whom your son gave his life. He saved many lives that day, and he was carrying me to safety when a bullet struck him in the heart and he died instantly. He often talked about you, and your love for art."

The young man held out his package. "I know this isn't much. I'm not really a great artist, but I think your son would have wanted you to have this."

The father opened the package. It was a portrait of his son, painted by the young man. He stared in awe at the way the soldier had captured the personality of his

---

[61] Retrieved from http://www.jaredstory.com/story_of_a_son.html. According to writers at www.snopes.com (February 2008), this tale is folklore that has been popularized on the Internet but is based on a story that was originally published in 1954. Over the years, this tale has been modified to include characters and events that are not present in the original publication and is published online as having an unknown author.

son in the painting. The father was so drawn to the eyes that his own eyes welled up with tears.

He thanked the young man and offered to pay him for the picture. "Oh, no sir, I could never repay what your son did for me. It's a gift."

The father hung the portrait over his mantle. Every time visitors came to his home he took them to see the portrait of his son before he showed them any of the other great works he had collected.

The man died a few months later. There was to be a great auction of his paintings. Many influential people gathered, excited over seeing the great paintings and having an opportunity to purchase one for their collection On the platform sat the painting of the son.

The auctioneer pounded his gavel. "We will start the bidding with this picture of the son. Who will bid for this picture?"

There was silence. Then a voice in the back of the room shouted, "We want to see the famous paintings. Skip this one."

But the auctioneer persisted, "Will someone bid for this painting? Who will start the bidding? $100, $200?"

Another voice shouted angrily, "We didn't come to see this painting. We came to see the Van Goghs, the Rembrandts. Get on with the real bids!" But still the auctioneer continued, "The son! The son! Who'll take the son?"

Finally, a voice came from the very back of the room. It was the longtime gardener of the man and his son. "I'll give $10 for the painting." Being a poor man, it was all he could afford.

"We have $10, who will bid $20?" "Give it to him for $10. Let's see the masters." "$10 is the bid, won't someone bid $20?" The crowd was becoming angry. They didn't want the picture of the son. They wanted the more worthy investments for their collections. The auctioneer pounded the gavel. "Going once, twice, SOLD for $10!"

A man sitting on the second row shouted, "Now let's get on with the collection!" The auctioneer laid down his gavel, "I'm sorry, the auction is over."

"What about the paintings?"

"I am sorry. When I was called to conduct this auction, I was told of a secret stipulation in the will. I was not allowed to reveal that stipulation until this time. Only the painting of the son would be auctioned. Whoever bought that painting would inherit the entire estate, including the paintings. The man who took the son gets everything!"

God gave his Son 2,000 years ago to die on a cruel cross. Much like the auctioneer, His message today is, "The Son, the Son, who'll take the Son?" Because you see, whoever takes the Son gets everything.

Yes. Whoever takes the Son gets everything. The moment we take Jesus, we get healing. The moment we take Jesus, we get prosperity. The moment we take Jesus, we get peace. The moment we take Jesus, we get victory. The moment we take Jesus, we get love. The moment we take Jesus, we get wisdom for every situation. The moment we take Jesus, we get everything He died and rose again to give us! Jesus is a package deal! The very moment you take Him, you get it all!

I know what many of you are thinking: "*I took Jesus, but where is my healing? I took Jesus, but why am I still in debt? I took Jesus, but why is there strife in my home? I took Jesus, but why ...?*" My question to you is, Have you received?

What Does It Mean to Receive?

In a word, receive means "take."[62]

"*What? Is it that easy?*" you ask.

Yes, Beloved, it is. Imagine a friend of yours asks you for twenty dollars. "Sure, it's on the table," you say. As far as you are concerned, that twenty dollars is his; he asked you for it, and you said yes and told him where it was. The next day your friend asks you for twenty dollars again. You look on the table and see that the twenty dollars you gave him yesterday is still there. What happened? Your friend never took it. The twenty dollars belongs to him, but it is just sitting there, unclaimed and unused, of no avail to him because he did not take it.

It is the same way with God and His children. There are many things available to us in the Kingdom of God, and they are all ours for the taking, for it is our Father's good pleasure to give us the Kingdom[63]. The problem is, we aren't taking them, so they are all just sitting there—unclaimed, unused, and of no avail to us.

God has already provided everything we will ever need. Remember the *Sozo Package*? It's all sitting there in His Word - in His Kingdom - waiting for us to take it! And He's given us total access to it. In Mark 11:24, Jesus is in the middle of explaining to His disciples how to get their prayers answered. He explains that whatever things you desire, when you pray, "believe that ye receive them, and ye shall have them" (KJV). Another

---

[62]   *Strong's Greek*, word 2893.

[63]   See Luke 12:32.

way of saying this would be "Whatever things you desire, when you pray, believe that you *take* them, and you will *have* them."

The first thing we must realize, however, is there is nothing we can do to deserve anything that God has for us. We cannot work for it. We cannot earn it. We must simply *receive* it, or *take* it - believing that it is God's pleasure to give it to us and knowing that God has pleasure in the prosperity of His children (Psalm 35:27). It is coming to this realization that will make the difference between entering into relationship with God or enduring religion created by man. The key will be to receive God's salvation, which includes all the blessings bestowed by God on men in Christ through the Holy Spirit.

How to Receive Salvation

If you are a born-again believer, you may be tempted to skip over this section. However, I encourage you to read this section in its entirety. You may be thinking, *"Why do I need to learn about how to receive salvation? I am already saved."* This may be true. However, many Christians - as born-again and heaven-bound as they may be - are comfortable with (and perhaps even resigned to) the notion that they have to go through hell to get to get there. While this may be the thought process and experience of many Christians, God never intended for it to be our reality.

Jesus came to give us life and life more abundantly (John 10:10). Yes, we will experience tribulation in this world, but we can rejoice, for Jesus has overcome the world![64] If we are born again, Jesus lives in us, and greater is He that is in us than he that is in the world (I John 4:4). So, we do not have to go through hell to get to Heaven. We are victorious! We are more than conquerors![65] Thanks be to God who *always* causes us to

---

[64] See John 16:33.

[65] See Romans 8:37.

triumph in Christ (2 Corinthians 2:14, emphasis added)! Unfortunately, religious thinking has kept people from living this truth.

Religion has taught us that in order to get saved (or to receive salvation), we must first confess that we are sinners. But that is not what the scripture says. Romans 10:9 says, "That if thou shalt confess with thy mouth the Lord Jesus, and shalt believe in thine heart that God hath raised Him from the dead, thou shalt be saved." This scripture does *not* say "That if thou shalt confess with thy mouth that thou art a sinner and ask God for forgiveness …" No, it says, "That if thou shalt confess with thy mouth *the Lord Jesus* …" Let us pause to examine Romans 10:9 in detail.

<u>That if thou shalt confess with thy mouth …</u>

The word "confess" in Romans 10:9 means "to say the same with another," or to "assent, accord, to agree with," and to "concede, admit, confess."[66] So confessing the Lord Jesus is nothing more than agreeing with the Word about who Jesus is and saying it. When you enter into agreement with God's Word about who Jesus is, you agree that Jesus is who God says He is and that Jesus did what God said He did.

Jesus is God's Son—God's only begotten Son—whom He gave to die on the cross for our sins. He loved us so much and wanted us to live the wonderful life with Him that He had planned for us before the beginning of time. The only way He could make that possible for us was to send His Son, Jesus, the only acceptable sacrifice for our sins. The only way we can live that wonderful life that He planned for us—both on earth and into eternity—is to believe on His Son, Jesus. For God so loved the world that He gave His only begotten Son, that whosoever believeth in Him should not perish but have everlasting life (John 3:16).

---

[66] James Strong, *The Exhaustive Concordance of the Bible*, (New York: Hunt &Eaton, 1890), retrieved from http://biblehub.com/greek/3670.htm.

Isaiah 53:3–12 paints a very clear picture of what Jesus endured on our behalf:

	New Living Translation	The Message
3	He was despised and rejected—a man of sorrows, acquainted with deepest grief. We turned our backs on Him and looked the other way. He was despised, and we did not care.	He was looked down on and passed over, a man who suffered, who knew pain firsthand. One look at Him and people turned away. We looked down on Him, thought He was scum.
4	Yet it was our weaknesses He carried; it was our sorrows that weighed Him down. And we thought His troubles were a punishment from God, a punishment for His own sins!	But the fact is, it was *our* pains He carried – *our* disfigurements, all the things wrong with *us*. We thought He brought it on Himself, that God was punishing Him for His own failures.
5	But He was pierced for our rebellion, crushed for our sins. He was beaten so we could be whole. He was whipped so we could be healed.	But it was our sins that did that to Him, that ripped and tore and crushed Him – *our sins*! He took the punishment, and that made us whole. Through His bruises we get healed.
6	All of us, like sheep, have strayed away. We have left God's paths to follow our own. Yet the LORD laid on Him the sins of us all.	We're all like sheep who've wandered off and gotten lost. We've all done our own thing, gone our own way. And GOD has piled all our sins, everything we've done wrong on Him, on Him.

7	He was oppressed and treated harshly, yet He never said a word. He was led like a lamb to the slaughter. And as a sheep is silent before the shearers, He did not open His mouth.	He was beaten, He was tortured, but He didn't say a word. Like a lamb taken to be slaughtered and like a sheep being sheared, He took it all in silence.
8	Unjustly condemned, He was led away. No one cared that He died without descendants, that His life was cut short in midstream. But He was struck down for the rebellion of My people.	Justice miscarried, and He was led off – and did anyone really know what was happening? He died without a thought for His own welfare, beaten bloody for the sins of My people.
9	He had done no wrong and had never deceived anyone. But He was buried like a criminal; He was put in a rich man's grave.	They buried Him with the wicked, threw Him in a grave with a rich man, even though He'd never hurt a soul or said one word that wasn't true.
10	But it was the LORD'S good plan to crush Him and cause Him grief. Yet when His life is made an offering for sin, He will have many descendants. He will enjoy a long life, and the LORD's good plan will prosper in His hands.	Still, it's what GOD had in mind all along, to crush Him with pain. The plan was that *He give Himself* as an offering for sin so that He'd see life come from it – life, life, and more life. And GOD's plan will deeply prosper through Him.

11	When He sees all that is accomplished by His anguish, He will be satisfied. AND BECAUSE OF HIS EXPERIENCE, MY RIGHTEOUS SERVANT WILL MAKE IT POSSIBLE FOR MANY TO BE COUNTED RIGHTEOUS, FOR HE WILL BEAR ALL THEIR SINS.	Out of that terrible travail of soul, He'll see that it's worth it and will be glad He did it. THROUGH WHAT HE EXPERIENCED, MY RIGHTEOUS ONE, MY SERVANT, WILL MAKE MANY "RIGHTEOUS ONES," AS HE HIMSELF CARRIES THE BURDEN OF THEIR SINS.
12	I will give Him the honors of a victorious soldier, because He exposed Himself to death. He was counted among the rebels. He bore the sins of many and interceded for rebels (emphasis added).	Therefore I'll reward Him extravagantly – the best of everything, the highest honors - because He looked death in the face and didn't flinch, because He embraced the company of the lowest. HE TOOK ON HIS OWN SHOULDERS THE SIN OF THE MANY, HE TOOK UP THE CAUSE OF ALL THE BLACK SHEEP (emphasis added).

SE-LAH! Pause and think about *THAT! THAT'S* who Jesus is! *THAT'S* what He did! That's what He did for *YOU!* That's what He did for *ME!* And all God wants us to do is *receive* Him. Hallelujah!

Can you come into agreement with that? To agree with someone is to be of one mind with someone, to harmonize in opinion with someone, and to live in concord, or without contention with, someone.[67] Can you

---

67   Webster.

be of one mind with God and live in concord with Him, saying that Jesus is God's Son and that He died in your place so you wouldn't have to? That He took sickness, poverty, and grief upon Himself so you could live free from it? That He took the judgment of God upon Himself so you could escape judgment and condemnation? He died to make you righteous *the very moment* you believe in Him so you can enjoy everything that God has for you. Salvation is just the beginning. If you can believe Him for your salvation, you can believe Him for everything else!

<u>... the Lord Jesus ...</u>

As the One who gave His life for you, Jesus wants to be the Lord of your life. "Lord" in this sense means "supreme in authority" or "master."[68] Jesus does not want to be Lord of your life so He can be a hard taskmaster. On the contrary, He wants to be Lord of your life so He can teach you how to enjoy life to the fullest! Jesus said in John 10:10, "I am come that [you] might have life, and that [you] might have it more abundantly." Listen to His heart as He extends this invitation to you:

> *Come to Me. Get away with Me and you'll recover your life.*
> *I'll show you how to take a real rest. Walk with Me*
> *and work with Me—watch how I do it.*
> *Learn the unforced rhythms of grace. I won't lay*
> *anything heavy or ill-fitting on you.*
> *Keep company with Me and you'll learn to live freely*
> *and lightly (Matthew 11:28-29 MSG).*
> *Love, Jesus*

Who wouldn't want a Lord like that?

<u>... and shalt believe in thine heart ...</u>

To believe is to have a firm persuasion of anything. In this scripture, "believe" means "to trust, to place full confidence in, to rest upon with faith."[69] When you believe with your heart, you believe with your innermost being - not with your mind or even your feelings. You believe with your very spirit—the essence of who you are. Believing in this manner is very important, as it is a vital part of receiving God's promises.

---

[68] James Strong, *The New Strong's Expanded Dictionary of Bible Words*, Greek word 2962 (Nashville, Tennessee: Thomas Nelson, 2001).

[69] Webster.

… that God has raised Him from the dead …

Part of receiving salvation is believing in your innermost being—beyond what your mind can comprehend—that God raised Jesus from the dead. To most people, it is impossible to conceive that someone could be raised from the dead—especially after three days—which is why your believing is so important. To believe that God has raised Jesus from the dead is to believe that Jesus is alive and well, and that He has accomplished all that God sent Him to accomplish on our behalf. To believe that God has raised Jesus from the dead is to believe that Jesus has taken the punishment that we should have taken, that our sins are no longer held against us, and that we are in right standing with God—eligible to receive all of His promises.

… thou shalt be saved!

Are you ready to receive? It is as simple as believing in your heart and speaking with your mouth that Jesus is the Son of God and that God raised Him from the dead. This invitation is extended to unsaved people and saved people alike. I know you must be asking, *"How can you invite saved people to receive salvation?"* Some people have sincerely received Jesus (i.e., gotten saved) but endure religion rather than enjoy salvation. Perhaps you have been praying, going to church, working in ministries, volunteering, and doing a lot of the "right" things in trying to live right—but something is still missing. You can't find your joy. You don't feel peace. You're running in circles. You're worn out. You're at your wits' end. Maybe the reason is that you have only received a portion of your salvation—the portion that allows you to get into Heaven. Sure, you have secured a place in Heaven, but you spend too much time going through hell here on earth. Salvation is so much more!

> You want healing? It's in there!
> Freedom from oppression? It's in there!
> Debt-freedom? It's in there!

Restoration? It's in there!

Love? It's in there!

Joy? Peace? It's in there!

Like the son in the Prego commercial, I lift the spoon to your lips—the spoon of salvation, inviting you to taste and see that the Lord is good.[70]

No matter who you are, if you are ready to receive salvation, pray these words:

> Thank You, Jesus, for dying on the cross for my sins. Thank you for dying in my place that I may live. I believe that you are the Son of God and that You rose on the third day. I make you the Lord of my life. Thank you for making every provision for me that I will ever need. I receive it all by faith. I renounce my sin, the devil, and everything He stands for. I turn to You. Thank You for teaching me how to live the abundant life and to receive everything God has for me. Amen!

Hallelujah!

Welcome to the Family!

If you prayed that prayer in sincerity, you are born again! You are a child of God! Now that you have received Jesus, God's Holy Spirit lives inside of you. But this is just the beginning!

There is new power available to you to learn and to maintain all that you have just received. It is by and through this power that you will be able to live out all that God has given you. He has made this power

---

[70]   See Psalm 34:8.

available to you through the baptism of His precious Holy Spirit *if* you would like to receive it. He will not force you to receive it. Though the Holy Spirit lives inside You, He will not just overtake you. You must *receive* the baptism of the Holy Spirit just as you *received* salvation through Jesus. To learn more about the Holy Spirit and the power that the baptism of the Holy Spirit affords you, see Appendix C.

Ask God to lead you to a Bible-believing church where you will be taught the Word of God without compromise, where you can grow in the Lord and in the things of God. Welcome to the family!

I've Received—Now What?

If you prayed that prayer but do not see an immediate change or feel any different—rejoice anyway! This is where faith comes in. Actually, faith came in when you decided to receive Jesus. It takes faith to believe that Someone who never committed sin *became sin* so you could *be made righteous* with no doing of your own. It takes faith to believe that Someone who was buried for three days was raised from the dead. It takes faith to believe that Someone could wipe your slate absolutely clean so your past doesn't even matter. So don't let this faith talk scare you. You are already on your way!

Faith is an extension of your belief. Faith is the expression of what you believe even – and especially - when you don't see manifestation of what you believe. For example: *I believe this chair (that I have never sat in before) will support me when I sit down.* The [faith] expression of my belief is that I sit in the chair even though I have no proof that that chair will support me. I sit in the chair because *I believe* it will support me. If I didn't believe the chair would support me, I would not sit in it. My faith expression (i.e., sitting down) is proof of my belief (i.e., the chair will support me).

When you receive salvation, you believe that you have been made the righteousness of God. You may not see or feel anything that supports what you believe. In fact, you may feel the exact opposite. You may feel a tremendous temptation to do that thing that you used to do. Don't let that throw you. Remember, that is not the real you anymore. You are a new creature. It may take your mind and body some time to catch up, but in the meantime, the faith expression of your belief is that you thank God for saving you even though you may not feel any different. You thank God because you *believe* that you are a new creature and that you are the righteousness of God. Your faith expression (i.e., thanking God) is proof of your belief (i.e. that you are a new creature and that you have been made the righteousness of God).

As you continue to demonstrate faith expressions regarding your being a new creature and having been made righteous through Jesus, manifestations will begin to appear. You and others around you will notice that you don't act the way you used to act, or things don't bother you the way they used to, or that you don't have the desire to do the things you used to do. The key is to believe with your spirit—with your innermost being—beyond what your eyes, mind, or feelings dictate or comprehend. Then confess what you believe (i.e., speak your agreement with what God's Word says). That is when you begin to see manifestations of the promises of God in your life.

How to Receive the Promises of God

Receive the promises of God the same way you receive salvation and the same way you receive forgiveness; believe in your innermost being—beyond what your eyes, mind, and feelings can comprehend—and receive the promises. Take them as your own! Start by believing, rehearsing, and receiving His love for you.

Rehearse God's love by studying scriptures about His love,[71] thinking about them over and over again throughout your day. Read them out loud so you will hear them audibly and not just in your head. Memorize them. Study them over and over again. Make them personal by applying them to yourself. For instance, when reading John 3:16, make it personal by putting yourself in the scripture: "For God so loved [your name] that He gave His only begotten Son Jesus, that if [your name] would believe in Him, [your name] should not perish, but have everlasting life" (John 3:16).

Realize that if you were the only person on earth, God would have sent Jesus just for you. He spared not His own Son but delivered Him up for you; how shall He not with Him also freely give you all things?[72] Take God's love personally. Yes, God loves everybody, but there is power in realizing how much He loves *you*. As you meditate on how much God loves you, how He gave His *best* for *you,* and how He gave His *only* for *you*—you grow in the knowledge and understanding of who God is; God is *LOVE!*[73]

As you begin to grow in confidence of God's love for you, you begin to realize that it is in His very nature to bless you, to bestow good things upon you, to empower you to succeed, and to give you everything you need:

> By His divine power, God has given us everything we need for living a godly life. We have received all of this by coming to know Him, the One who called us to Himself by means of His marvelous glory and excellence. And because of His glory and excellence, He has given us great and precious promises. These are the promises that enable you to share His divine nature and escape the world's corruption caused by human desires" (2 Peter 1:3–4 NLT).

---

[71]   See Appendix A.

[72]   See Romans 8:32.

[73]   See 1 John 4:8.

The Message translation of the Bible says that these promises are our tickets to participation in the life of God after we turn our backs on a world corrupted by lust.[74] Some of you may be balking at the idea of participating in the life of God or living a godly life. You may think that a godly lifestyle is too strict a lifestyle, too stifling a lifestyle, or too boring a lifestyle. Or maybe you think that a godly lifestyle is too demanding a lifestyle. Au contraire, my friend! Listen to Jesus' invitation to you:

> *Come to Me, all you who labor and are heavy-laden and*
> *overburdened, and I will cause you to rest. [I will ease and relieve and*
> *refresh your souls.] Take My yoke upon you and learn of Me, for I am*
> *gentle (meek) and humble (lowly) in heart, and you will find rest (relief and*
> *ease and refreshment and recreation and blessed quiet) for your souls. For*
> *My yoke is wholesome (useful, good—not harsh, hard, sharp, or pressing,*
> *but comfortable, gracious, and pleasant), and My burden is*
> *light and easy to be borne*
> *(Matthew 11:28–30 Amplified, Classic Edition).*

God did not intend for us to live stressful lives. On the contrary, He wanted us to have peaceful lives. He wanted us to have prosperous lives.

> For I know the thoughts that I think toward you, saith the Lord, thoughts of peace, and not of evil, to give you an expected end. (Jeremiah 29:11 KJV)

> Beloved, I pray that you may prosper in all things and be in health, just as your soul prospers. (3 John 2 NKJV)

> … Let the LORD be magnified, which hath pleasure in the prosperity of His servant. (Psalm 35:27 KJV)

---

74   See 1 Peter 1:4 MSG.

The word translated as "peace" in Jeremiah 29:11 means "safety, welfare, health, prosperity, rest, and wholeness."[75] Likewise, the word translated as "prosper" in 3 John 2 means "to succeed in reaching; to have a prosperous journey."[76] Prosperity means "to have completeness, wholeness, soundness, health, and peace."[77] In other words, prosperity is more than just having riches. It is being prosperous in every area of your life. God does not want to see us struggle. He thinks peace toward us. Why? To *give* us an expected end!

What expected end? Peace! Safety, welfare, health, prosperity, rest, and wholeness! That is His expected end for us! He doesn't just think about us and let it go at that. You know how people say, "I've been thinking about you," but that's all they did? They didn't call you, visit you, or do anything to give you any indication that they were thinking about you? God is not that way. He has purpose in everything He does. He thinks about us with the intention, the desire, and the delight to give us everything He has for us! He created us to have good lives, and being the loving God that He is, He arranged paths for us and made them ready so we could live those good lives:

> For we are God's [own] handiwork (His workmanship) recreated in Christ Jesus, [born anew] that we may do those good works which God predestined (planned beforehand) for us [taking paths which He prepared ahead of time], that we should walk in them [living the good life which He prearranged and made ready for us to live]" (Ephesians 2:10 Amplified, Classic Edition).

So if God thinks thoughts of peace toward us to *give* us an expected end—the good and prosperous life He desires for us to enjoy—and has

---

75 *Strong's Hebrew*, word 7965.

76 *Strong's Greek*, word 2137.

77 *Strong's Hebrew*, word 7695.

prepared paths for us ahead of time so we can live the good and prosperous life He desires for us to enjoy, how do we *take* those paths that we might *receive* the expected end?

Is it fair to say that when you *take* a path, you *receive* the direction the path provides? Consider this with me: When you take a path, you go where it leads you. You could choose to get off the path, or to go on a different path. But instead you stick with this path. Therefore, you receive, or accept, the direction that this path provides. In the same way, God wants us to receive, accept, or take the direction that He provides. He has provided us direction through His prearranged paths so we can reach the expected end—the good, prosperous life He planned for us from before the foundation of the world.

So the question becomes, how do we take these paths? We find our answer in Matthew 6:33:

> "But seek (aim at and strive after) first of all [God's] kingdom
> and His righteousness (His way of doing and being right) …"
> (Amplified, Classic Edition).

When we aim at and strive after God's way of doing and being right (i.e., living the godly life), and we make it our first priority to do so, we are taking the paths that He has laid before us. Understand that to "aim at and strive after" does not mean to toil and to stress. Rather it means to set your eyes on your target and determine that nothing will distract you from hitting that target.

With regard to living the godly life, Jesus tells us we are to lock our focus on Him: we are to learn of Him, to walk with Him, and work with Him—to watch how He does it.[78] Living a godly life is as simple as getting in the Word (i.e., studying the Bible) and beholding Jesus.

---

[78] See Matthew 11:28 Amplified Bible, Classic Edition.

"What?" you exclaim. *"But the scripture says to strive after His way of doing and being right. It says to work with Him. That sounds like hard work to me!"*

Again, to "aim at and strive after" means to set your eyes on your target and determine that nothing will distract you from reaching that target. To work with Jesus is simply to let Him have His way. Get rid of your resistance and just let Him have free reign. When He tells you to do something, do it. When He tells you not to do something, don't do it. When He tells you to stop doing something, stop doing it! Work with Him! That's not hard.

I repeat: living a godly life is as simple as getting in the Word and beholding Jesus. Behold means "to look at." The more we behold Jesus in the Word, the more clearly He appears to us. The Bible says that when He appears, we see Him as He is and we become like Him.[79] We become what we behold.

"Surely there's got to be more to it than that!" you say. *"There's got to be more to it than just beholding Jesus in the Word!"*

I say to you, let the Word do the work. Read the Word, behold Jesus (by meditating on the Word), and watch the Word bring about changes in your life.[80] God's Word will change you effortlessly if you take the effort to put God's Word in your heart.[81] Behold Jesus: His yoke is easy and His burden is light. He will teach you how to walk in the unforced rhythms of grace, and you will be changed into His image from glory to glory.[82]

God knows the thoughts that He thinks toward you to give you an expected end—the good and prosperous life He desires for you to enjoy.

---

[79] See 1 John 3:2.

[80] See "Meditate the Word" on page 53.

[81] Andrew Wommack, from his teaching *Effortless Change*, available for download and for purchase at www.awmi.net.

[82] See Matthew 11:29–30 KJV; MSG; 2 Corinthians 3:18.

Will you receive the direction He gives you in His Word so that expected end can manifest in your life?

How to Receive Forgiveness of Sins

I hear the Spirit of God say that there are many Christians who have not received their forgiveness. Because they have not received their forgiveness, they are walking round under a cloud of guilt, shame, and condemnation, allowing the devil to rob them of blessings that already belong to them and to hinder them from reaching their expected end. They are constantly "repenting" for their sins ... constantly telling God they are sorry for something He has already forgiven them for.

Repent does not mean "to apologize." Rather, repent means "to turn from the wrong way of doing things and turn to the right way of doing things." In other words, turn from your way of doing things and turn to God's way of doing things. Turn from sin. Turn to Righteousness, Who is Jesus.

If you are one who is constantly telling God you are sorry for sins you have committed ... constantly reminding Him of something He has already forgiven you for ... constantly reminding Him of something that He has chosen not to remember any more - I speak to you right now in the Name of Jesus and say, "**Stop it!**"

God loves you! There is *no condemnation* to those who are in Christ Jesus. That means there is no more judgment against you! God sent Jesus to this world not to condemn you but to save you. Put your eyes on this:

> There is therefore now *no condemnation* to them which are in
> Christ Jesus, who walk not after the flesh, but after the Spirit
> (Romans 8:1, emphasis added).

For God sent *not* his Son into the world to condemn the world;
but that the world through him might be saved.
He that believeth on Him is *NOT CONDEMNED* ... (John
3:17–18a, emphasis added).

Like healing, restoration, and prosperity, forgiveness is one of the
finished works of Jesus Christ. It is something Jesus accomplished for you
when He died and rose again. All you have to do is *receive* it. TAKE it!
If you are one who has been walking with the Lord but has been bound
by guilt, shame, and condemnation, you can be free today. Receive your
forgiveness by praying these words:

Lord, thank You for forgiving me. I receive my forgiveness right
now, in the Name of Jesus. I take it, and I don't let it go. I no
longer walk in guilt. I no longer walk in shame. I no longer walk
in condemnation. I walk in the liberty that Christ died to give me.

Anytime I feel the care of those feelings welling up inside
me, I determine right now to cast that care onto You immediately,
and I won't take it back, for You care for me.[83] I receive Your love. I
believe, I receive that You are pleased with me, for according to John
17:23, You love me just as much as You love Jesus. Thank You, Jesus!
I am forgiven! *I AM FORGIVEN!*

Now that you have received God's forgiveness, forgive yourself
and be free.

What Do I Do When I Mess Up?

When you mess up—and we all do—run to the One Who loves you. First
John 2:1 tells us that when we sin, we have an Advocate, and His name

---

[83]   See 1 Peter 5:7.

is Jesus. An advocate is someone who pleads the cause of anyone before a judge.[84] When we mess up … when we sin … when we fall short - Jesus is already pleading our case, telling God that we are covered by His blood and that He has already paid the price for us. The next verse (1 John 2:2) tells us that Jesus was the propitiation for our sins. In other words, He was the vessel who pacified God's anger even though God had every reason to be angry with us. And He reconciled us to God—assuaging God's wrath and putting Him in the mood to be eternally gracious toward us.[85] When Jesus died on the cross, He was the perfect sacrifice—the *perfect price paid*—for every sin that had been committed and that would ever be committed by anyone past, present, and future.[86]

Religion has taught us that we need to confess our sins to be forgiven. While we do need to confess our sins, the fact of the matter is that God has already forgiven us. First John 1:9 says that if we confess our sins, God is faithful and just to forgive us our sins and to cleanse us from all unrighteousness. Why? Because He has already forgiven us. He has already cleansed us. He forgave us when He raised Jesus from the dead over 2000 years ago. Forgiveness is there waiting for us. Cleansing is there waiting for us. But we must *take* it. Believe that you receive it, and you shall have it (Mark 11:24).

We do not confess our sins to get God to forgive us. Rather, we confess our sins because we are forgiven.[87]

What?

Yes. Remember, the word confess means "to say the same thing." The word confess in the context of this book means "to say the same thing God says." So when we confess our sins, we say the same thing about our sins that God says about our sins:

---

[84]   See *Strong's Greek*, word 3875.

[85]   See *Strong's Greek*, word 2434; also see Webster.

[86]   See Hebrews 10:10, 12, 14; 1 John 2:2.

[87]   Meditate on the Forgiven Scriptures listed in Appendix B.

This [act, word, thought, etc.] is sin.

According to Psalm 103:3, You forgive all my iniquities. This [act, word, thought, etc.] is forgiven.

Thank You, Father.

I receive my forgiveness in Jesus' Name.

Then we walk free of condemnation[88] and do as Jesus instructed the woman who had been caught in adultery: "Go, and sin no more" (John 8:10–11). That is not to say, "Be perfect or else!" No, that is to say, "Now that you have turned to God in this area of your life, continue to seek Him. Continue to follow Him. He is Spirit.[89] If you walk after the Spirit, you will not satisfy the lust of the flesh."[90]

God has forgiven you. Jesus has set you free from the dominion of sin. So I charge you: BE FORGIVEN! BE FREE! Believe you receive and TAKE your forgiveness! TAKE your freedom! IN JESUS' NAME!

When you receive your forgiveness and walk in the freedom that Jesus died and rose again to give you, you position yourself to see greater manifestation of God's promises in your life.

---

[88] See Romans 8:1.

[89] See John 4:24.

[90] See Galatians 5:16.

Part III

How Do I See Manifestations of the Promises of God?

You may be thinking, *"All of this talk of believing and receiving is wonderful. But really, how do I see manifestations of the promises of God? I don't just want to believe for my healing. I want to BE healed! I don't just want to believe that my bills are paid. I want my bills to BE PAID OFF! I don't just want to believe for my family's salvation. I want to SEE my family saved! I don't want to just believe for a job. I want to HAVE a job! I don't just want to believe for a car. I want to DRIVE the car! I don't want to just believe for my mate. I want to ENJOY my mate!"*

I understand. If you are like me, there are several things that you have believed for but, for whatever reason, have not seen manifest in your life. Admittedly, I have not yet mastered the art of receiving the promises of God, but I am growing more proficient every day. As one of my favorite Bible teachers says, "I haven't arrived, but I've left!"

I am grateful to God for the people that He has brought into my life to teach me how to receive the manifestation of His promises. They have taught me not just through instruction but also through example. I bless each and every one of them in the name of the Lord. To see their tenacity in following the Lord and making the Word first place and supreme authority in their lives has been encouraging and life-changing. I am particularly grateful to and for my pastors, who have taken God's call seriously to "take a group of people and disciple them intensely in the

Word of God, teaching them an uncommon faith and helping them to stand victoriously in life."[91]

However, if I am telling the whole truth, I must admit that it has also been frustrating. Frustrating in the sense that I feel like an athlete is who is in training. I feel as if I am being pushed to the limit. Sometimes it feels as though the goal is so far out of reach that I will never make it. I get tired and want to quit. At times I even get downright angry! My spiritual coaches have no pity on me. If anything, they turn up the heat! And they don't even know it! They are just being who they are—faithful and consistent in their walk with the Lord, setting an example of victory that is second to none on this present-day earth, as far as I am concerned.

In a funny sort of way, the frustration leads to a greater inspiration to go deeper and deeper and higher and higher. It was in 2012 that I first felt this degree of frustration. I was in North Carolina and had recently been introduced to teachings that I have shared with you in this book. At this point, I was listening to a series entitled The Goodness of God, taught by Pastor George Pearsons and Sister Gloria Copeland.[92] I was disturbed when, whereas I usually absorb the Word of God like a sponge, I was having trouble absorbing this Word. It was as if I could feel the seeds falling onto the soil of my heart, but instead of them sinking down into the soil, they just sat on top.

I wondered why it seemed so hard to receive the message that God is good—especially when I already knew it! After all, I had been walking closely with the Lord for many years. I had even been disinvited from churches recently because of my love of and stand on the Word. Why was it so difficult for me to receive this Word that God is good?

The frustration I felt prompted me to say, "Lord, I *have* to sit under this teaching!" I was ready to pack up and leave right then, but God had other plans. I packed up all right, but it would be a two-year journey before

---

[91] Commission Statement at Eagle Mountain International Church in Newark, Texas.

[92] Available for purchase at www.KCM.org.

I would arrive to physically sit under the teaching that I so desired. God led me on a meandering (and much-needed) journey to bring me to the place where I am now—physically, mentally, and spiritually. I am happy to say that I am seeing the move of God more strongly than I ever have. I have a greater expectation than I have ever had to see the manifestation of God's promises in my life.

So the question remains: how do I see the manifestation of God's promises in my life?

Principles for Receiving the Manifestation of God's Promises

God has given me the following principles for receiving the manifestation of His promises. While these principles can be considered core principles, they should not be considered comprehensive by any means:

I. Be Born Again

"Be born again" is another way of saying "Receive Jesus Christ as your Savior and Lord." Why is this a principle for receiving the manifestation of God's promises? Because *all* the promises of God *in Jesus* are yes![93] *All* of God's promises are found to be *YES … FULFILLED … DELIVERED.* Where? *In Christ*, the Anointed One, Who is Jesus. So if you want the guarantee of every one of God's promises fulfilled, you need to go where the promises are: In Christ—in Jesus.

How do you go where the promises are? Receive Jesus as your Savior and Lord. When you receive Jesus as your Savior and Lord, not only does He come live in you, but you are now *in Him.* Your past is wiped away. Second Corinthians 5:17 says, "…if anyone is *in Christ*, he is a new creation; *old things have passed away; behold, all things have become*

---

93 See 2 Corinthians 1:20 NKJV.

new" (NKJV, emphasis added). Your sins are washed away, never to be held against you again by your loving heavenly Father. As far as the east is from the west—that is how far God has separated your sins from you.[94] He has forgiven your sins and remembers them no more.[95] Why? Because He *loves* you! Look at this eye-opening picture of His unconditional love in Ephesians 2:4–5, 7 (Amplified, Classic Edition):

> … God—so rich is He in His mercy! Because of and in order to satisfy the great and wonderful and intense love with which He loved us,
>
> Even when we were dead (slain) by [our own] shortcomings and trespasses, He made us alive together in fellowship and in union with Christ; [He gave us the very life of Christ Himself, the same new life with which He quickened Him, for] it is by grace (His favor and mercy which you did not deserve) that you are saved (*delivered from judgment and made partakers of Christ's salvation*) …
>
> He did this that He might *clearly demonstrate* through the ages to come the immeasurable (limitless, surpassing) riches of His free grace, (His unmerited favor) in [His] kindness and goodness of heart toward us in Christ Jesus (emphasis added).

God is not angry at us. He is not holding any of our sins against us. He does not have ill will toward us—only love, kindness, and goodness of heart. He loves us so much that to satisfy His own intense love for us, He gave us His Son—while we were still caught up in our sin, and without any promise of a return on His investment.

---

94   See Psalm 103:12.

95   See Hebrews 8:12.

Jesus took all of the punishment for our sin when He was here on earth. He took it so we would not have to. He made the way for us to have eternal life with God our Father, who is in Heaven. But that's not all! Look at verse 5 above. Not only are those who have received Jesus as Savior delivered from judgment, but they are also made partakers of Christ's salvation. When Jesus endured the crucifixion and all that came with it, He made it possible for us to partake of His salvation and all that comes with it: *every* good thing that God had ever planned for us.[96] He came that we might have life and have it *more abundantly*.[97] All you have to do is receive Him for Who and all that He is, and you can have all that He came to give you. God is not a genie, mind you; but remember, whoever takes the Son gets everything.[98]

If you have not received Jesus as Savior and Lord, but you know there is more to life than what you are living and you want the manifestation of the good things God has promised in your life, won't you receive the Giver of every good and every perfect gift by receiving the Good and Perfect Gift Himself—Jesus Christ?[99]

Maybe you thought you had received salvation but you are realizing that you received religion instead. You received Jesus as your Savior, and you are confident that you are going to Heaven. However, without even knowing it, you have been working for your salvation rather than enjoying blessed relationship with your Heavenly Father and receiving all that He has for you. It's not too late. Won't you enter into blessed fellowship with your loving Father today and let Him show you His good pleasure of *giving* you the Kingdom?[100]

---

[96] See p. 26: Isaiah 53:3–11; See "What Is Salvation?" in part I of this book.

[97] See John 10:10.

[98] See "Who Will Take the Son?" on page 20.

[99] See James 1:17.

[100] See Luke 12:32.

If this is you and you want to receive Jesus as your Savior and Lord, or you want to enter into renewed fellowship with your Heavenly Father - it is my pleasure to lead you to the throne of grace.[101] Pray these words aloud:

> God,
>
> Thank you for sending Your Son, Jesus Christ, to die on the cross for me. He took the punishment that I should have taken and died the death that I should have died. Thank You for raising Him from the dead. He is alive today. Jesus, come live in me. I turn from my sin. I turn to You. I make You the Lord of my life. I cease from trying to earn what You have freely given me. I receive every good and every perfect gift that God has for me. I receive the abundant life that You came to give me. Teach me Your ways that I may walk in them. I thank You. In Jesus' Name. Amen.

Hallelujah!

Welcome to the Family!

If you prayed that prayer in sincerity, you are born again! You are a child of God! Now that you have received Jesus, God's Holy Spirit lives inside of you. But this is just the beginning!

There is new power available to you to learn and to maintain all that you have just received. It is by and through this power that you will be able to live out all that God has given you. He has made this power available to you through the baptism of His precious Holy Spirit *if* you would like to receive it. He will not force you to receive it. Though the Holy Spirit lives inside You, He will not just overtake you. You must *receive* the baptism of the Holy Spirit just as you *received* salvation through Jesus. To

---

101   See Hebrews 4:16.

learn more about the Holy Spirit and the power that the baptism of the Holy Spirit affords you, see Appendix C.

Ask God to lead you to a Bible-believing church where you will be taught the Word of God without compromise, where you can grow in the Lord and in the things of God. Welcome to the family!

Lest some of you think that I am offering Jesus merely as a means to have good things and am foregoing the relationship aspect, the holiness aspect, or the worship aspect—that is not what I am doing at all. Those who truly receive Jesus enter into relationship with Him. Through relationship, they become holy, just as He is holy.[102] Through relationship, they learn to worship Him in spirit and in truth.[103] Through relationship, they bring Him pleasure by receiving and enjoying His goodness, for *God has pleasure in the prosperity of His children* (Psalm 35:27).

Do not be afraid of receiving Jesus. Do not be afraid of receiving God's goodness. He will not give you anything that will hurt you or that will separate you from Him. So if you are thinking that nice things will separate you from God, that money will separate you from God, or that having loving relationships or walking in divine health will separate you from God—they won't—if you follow Him. Won't you receive Him today? It's not too late to pray the prayer above!

II.   Get In the Word

"Get in the Word" is another way of saying "read the Bible." The Bible is God's Word. It is God's Word to us. God speaks to us through His Word.

If you get in God's Word, God's Word will get in you, and the more faith you will have to speak His Word and to see His promises come to pass. Make up your mind that you believe the Bible is true. It is not a fairy tale to be read as though it is something fictitious or fantastical. It is

---

102   See 1 Peter 1:16.

103   See John 4:24.

not some grand piece of literature that merely records historical facts that happened a long time ago. It is God speaking to us. Now. In the present moment. God's Word is living, and it is powerful.[104] It is as pertinent today as it was the day it was written. It has an answer to every question and a solution to every problem. It is so full of life that you can read a scripture fifty times and get new revelation each time.

If you want to learn God's ways, you must heed His instruction. His instruction is in His Word.[105] If you want to walk in the paths God has for you, you must learn where those paths are. His paths are in His Word.[106] If you want to hear and recognize God's voice, you've got to get to know His voice. You come to recognize His voice by studying His Word. In God's Word is where you learn His vocabulary and His personality. In God's Word is where you learn to recognize the things that He says and the way that He says them, to the point that you will recognize a counterfeit when you hear it.[107]

For those of you who say the Bible is too hard to understand, ask God to lead you to a version that you can understand, and ask Him to speak to you while you read. God knows how to reach each one of us where we are. If we seek Him, we will find Him[108]. If we listen for His voice, we will hear Him, for His sheep hear His voice[109].

If you want to know what promises are available to you, you must learn what those promises are. God's promises are in His Word. When you learn His Word, you learn His promises. When you believe His Word, you believe His promises. When you speak His Word, you speak His promises. When you speak His promises in faith without doubting, you receive His promises.[110]

---

[104]　See Hebrews 4:12 NKJV.

[105]　See 2 Timothy 3:16–17.

[106]　See Psalm 119:105.

[107]　See John 10:4-5, 27

[108]　See Jeremiah 29:3

[109]　See John 10:27

[110]　See Mark 11:23-24

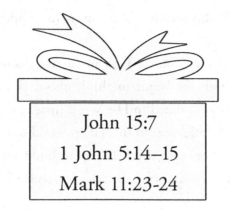

John 15:7
1 John 5:14–15
Mark 11:23-24

III.   Obey the Word

Obedience is the ultimate form of trust. Obedience shows God that you trust Him and that you believe what He says. Your obedience opens the door for God to manifest His promises in your life. If you want the Word of God (i.e., the promises of God) to come to pass in your life, you must obey God's Word.

James 1:22
John 2:5

IV.   Meditate the Word

If you want the Word of God and the promises of God to become real to you, you must meditate them—think on them constantly; speak them and mutter them aloud to yourself as you ponder them. "Meditate" means "to dwell on anything in thought; to turn or revolve any subject in the mind."[111] It also means "to murmur, to ponder, to mutter, and to speak."[112]

Meditating the Word of God in such a manner will help you to renew your mind—to begin to think about things the way God thinks about them as outlined in His Word instead of the way we have been trained by the influences in this fallen world to think about them. Meditating God's Word will also help you to build your faith and flush out unbelief, thus increasing your capacity to receive from God.

Romans 12:2 (ESV)
Romans 10:17 (KJV)

Meditating can be likened to a cow chewing her cud. Cows chew their food, swallow it, and then regurgitate it to chew it some more. This regurgitation process enables them to extract all of the nutrients and to digest the food properly. Experts say that cows spend about eight hours a day chewing their cud—rolling the bolus around in their mouths, making about thirty thousand chewing motions a day chewing cud alone. This

---

[111] Webster.

[112] *Strong's Hebrew*, word 1897.

does not include their initial food consumption, (i.e., chewing grass or hay), which equates to about ten thousand chewing motions a day.[113]

Believers can take a cue from these cows. Meditating on God's Word requires that we spend time with Him and in His Word. Sure, we may spend time reading the Bible—which is good—but this is like the cow's initial food consumption (only about ten thousand chewing motions as opposed to the thirty thousand when chewing cud). We should not just think about the Word while the Bible is open in front of us. Just as the cow's greater energy is spent in chewing the cud—regurgitating the food and rolling it around in her mouth—our greater energy should be spent in meditating the Word—constantly recalling the Word, thinking on the Word, rolling it around in our minds, speaking it aloud to ourselves, and getting it down into our hearts. (For it is only after we get the Word down in our hearts that it will come out of our mouths with power.[114])

Interestingly, experts say that cows chew their cud during times of rest. (Eight hours of rest. Imagine that!) This speaks to how we as believers should roll the Word of God around in our minds, speaking it aloud to ourselves—during times of resting in blessed fellowship with our Father (which should be all the time). We should not be toiling about trying to make things happen on our own or doing things in our own strength. We should be resting in God—meditating on His Word, renewing our minds, and increasing our capacity to receive from Him - watching His promises manifest in our lives as we obey Him. It is not by striving in our own strength that we succeed. Rather, it is by meditating on His Word.

---

[113] D. Amaral-Phillips, "Why Do Cattle Chew Their Cud?" accessed August 28, 2015, retrieved from afsdairy.ca.uky.edu/files/extension/nutrition/ Why_Do_Cattle_Chew_Their_Cud.pdf; Alicia McClure, "What Is Cud, and Why Do Cattle Chew It?" December 20, 2013,.retrieved from http://www. cattle-empire.net/blog/115/what-cud-and-why-do-cattle-chew-it.

[114] See Luke 6:45; Proverbs 18:21

Joshua 1:8

Did you know that abundant cud chewing is an indication that a cow is healthy and comfortable? It's true! Healthy, happy cows can be identified by how much they chew their cud.[115] There is much to be said for happy, healthy cows. They produce more milk and have more muscle than the other cows; thus they are stronger and more productive.[116]

Just as abundant cud-chewing is an indication that a cow is healthy and comfortable, abundant meditation on God's Word is an indication that a believer is healthy and joyful, for in God's presence there is fullness of joy.[117] Show me a believer who abundantly meditates God's Word, and I will show you a spiritually healthy, joyful believer. As is the case with healthy happy cows, healthy, joyful believers are stronger and more productive than their less healthy, less productive counterparts are. Believers who meditate God's Word are fruitful and prosperous.

---

[115]   Ibid.

[116]   Ibid.

[117]   See Psalm 16:11.

Psalm 1:2–3

V.   <u>Speak the Word</u>

If you want to see the promises of God manifest in your life, you must speak the Word *out loud*. Speaking God's Word out loud causes you to hear God's Word. Why is it important to hear God's Word? Because when we ask God for things, we need to have the faith to believe that He will do them. Speaking God's Word out loud causes us to hear God's Word, which causes faith to come:

> So then faith cometh by hearing, and hearing by the Word of God (Romans 10:17).

The more you hear God's Word, the more faith comes to you. The more faith comes to you, the more God's Word fills your heart. The more God's Word fills your heart, the more you will speak God's Word. The more you speak God's Word, the more you will release your faith. The more you release your faith, the more manifestation you will see.

> … The mouth speaks what the heart is full of. (Luke 6:45 NIV)

> … What you say flows from what is in your heart. (Luke 6:45 NLT)

… Out of the abundance of the heart his mouth speaks. (Luke 6:45 ESV)

If you want to see the promises of God manifest in your life, you must speak *God's* Word. God honors His Word. He does not obligate Himself to honor anybody else's word. So if you are speaking your own words to accomplish "mind over matter" or to merely to engage in positive thinking or speaking positively without having God's Word as your foundation, understand that God is not obligated to bring those things to pass. He watches over *His* Word.[118] However, *His* Word in *your* mouth is still *His* Word. The Word that you study and meditate, the Word that God speaks to you, the Word that you get down in your spirit and mix with faith—that is the Word that will come out of your mouth with power and that will accomplish what God (through you) has sent it out to accomplish.

Jeremiah 1:12
Isaiah 46:11b
Isaiah 55:11

VI.   Take God at His Word

If you want to receive the fullness of God's promises, you must take God at His Word. You must know that it is God's pleasure for you to have everything that He has promised. More importantly, you must know that God *never* goes back on His Word.

---

[118]   See Jeremiah 1:12 Amplified Bible, Classic Edition

> God is not a man, that He should lie; neither the son of man, that
> He should repent: hath He said, and shall He not do it? Or hath
> He spoken, and shall He not make it good? (Numbers 23:19 KJV).

It is a common saying where I come from that "faith begins where the will of God is known." We cannot have faith to receive anything from God until we know of a surety that it is His will for us to have it. Otherwise, we will pray in doubt—wondering if it is God's will. Or we will give up on praying for something that doesn't manifest when we think it should, saying that "it must not be God's will." Or we will cop out and place the responsibility on God, saying, "If it be God's will."

God has given us His Word, which is His will. It is our job to get in His Word to learn His will and then pray accordingly. If we pray according to His will, we know that He hears us and can be confident that He will give us what we have asked.

> And this is the confidence that we have in Him, that, if we ask
> any thing according to his will, He heareth us:
> And if we know that He hear us, whatsoever we ask, we know
> that we have the petitions that we desired of Him (I John 5:14-15).

It is God's pleasure to give us His Kingdom and everything in it. There are pleasures and perks and privileges that come with His Kingdom. He is not trying to hold anything back from us. He is trying to get it all to us, which is why He sent His Son, Jesus Christ, to die for us. He takes pleasure in our prosperity.

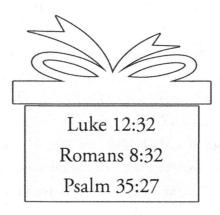

Luke 12:32

Romans 8:32

Psalm 35:27

VII.   <u>Rejoice over the Word</u>

If you want to see the promises of God in your life, rejoice over His Word to you. As is the case when receiving salvation, you may not see or feel an immediate change when you receive God's promises. Don't let that deter you. This is the time to rejoice!

Thanking God before you see the promise is your faith expression that lets Him know that you know you already have it. One of the greatest faith expressions we can offer is thanking God even though the promise has not manifested yet. Remember, faith is an extension of our belief. The moment we believe we *have received* the promise (past tense), we *have* it (present tense)—whether we can see it with our physical eyes or not. The moment we believe we have received is the moment we should begin rejoicing and sending praise up to our God. As wonderful as it is to see that thing that we've been believing for, the joy and peace come in believing for it.[119] It is the believing that increases our capacity to believe for more!

Mark 11:24
Romans 15:13

Principles for Holding On to the Manifestation of God's Promises

God has given me the following principles for holding on to His promises. Like the principles for receiving the manifestation of God's promises (see previous chapter), these principles can be considered core principles, but they should not be considered comprehensive by any means.

I.   Stay in the Word

If you want to hold on to the manifestation or the promise of the manifestation of what you are believing for, you must stay in the Word. There is something that happens between the "amen" of prayer and the manifestation of the answer to that prayer that tempts you to want to give up on what you are believing God for. It usually entails opposition, which requires you to stand; time, which requires you to persevere; and contrariness, which requires you to believe. It is during this time that you must do what you know to do. Let's review, shall we?

---

119   See Romans 15:13

If you are not born again, get born again.

If you are born again,

1. get in the Word
2. obey the Word
3. meditate the Word
4. speak the Word
5. take God at His Word, and
6. rejoice over the Word.

The principles for receiving the manifestation of God's promises are the same principles for holding on to the promises of God. You just have to do them more intensely when you are holding on to the manifestation or the promise of the manifestation. *Stay in the Word.* Continue to obey the Word. Continue to meditate the Word. Continue to speak the Word. The more proficient you become in these principles, the more effectively you will handle the forces that come against you, and the more quickly you will see the manifestations of what you are believing for.

II. <u>Stand on the Word (Don't Be Moved by What You See)</u>

The last thing the devil wants is for you to believe God. He knows that if you believe God, nothing is impossible to you.[120] Therefore, he does everything in his power to try to make you doubt God's Word. He wants you to think that God does not keep His promises, and he wants you to doubt God's love for you. But the devil is a liar! Know the following of a surety:

> God is not a man that He should lie; neither the son of man, that
> He should repent: hath He said, and shall He not do it? Or hath
> He spoken, and shall He not make it good? (Numbers 23:19)

---

[120] See Mark 9:23.

For the gifts and calling of God are irrevocable. (Romans 11:29 NKJV)

The enemy cannot afford to let the Word you hear become productive in your life. He knows that if it becomes productive in your life, he is in trouble. Therefore, he comes immediately to steal the Word that you have received, which is why it is important for you to get in the Word and *stay* in the Word by meditating it.[121] The more you meditate the Word, the more it takes root in you, and the more you get a vision on the inside of what God has said. Once you get a vision on the inside, it is only a matter of time before it manifests on the outside.

The degree to which you attend to the Word is the degree to which you will see results. The more time you give to the Word, the more fruit you will produce. Jesus described it as thirty-, sixty-, and a hundredfold [production]:

> And the seed that fell on good soil represents those who hear and accept God's word and produce a harvest of thirty, sixty, or even a hundred times as much as had been planted! (Mark 4:20 NLT)

> And these are they which are sown on good ground; such as hear the word, and receive it, and bring forth fruit, some thirtyfold, some sixty, and some an hundred (Mark 4:20 KJV).

If you want a thirtyfold return, give thirtyfold attention. If you want a sixtyfold return, give sixtyfold attention. But if you want a hundredfold return, give hundredfold attention.

We give attention to the Word by putting it in our eyes, in our ears, and in our mouths. We read the Word, listen to the Word, and speak the Word. We let the Word renew our minds to believe what God has spoken, to the point where *nothing* can sway us. We make up our minds to

---

121 Read the parable of the sower (Mark 4:1–32).

stand on the Word and not be moved (caused to change place or posture in any manner or by any means)[122] by what we see. We walk by faith and not by sight.[123] We determine, like the Apostle Paul, who endured many hardships, not to let any of the hardships we encounter move us away from following God.[124] We follow Jesus' instructions: "Do not be afraid, **only believe**" (Mark 5:36).

The degree to which we give attention to the Word is the degree to which we stand on the Word. The degree to which we stand on the Word is the degree to which we walk by faith. The degree to which we walk by faith is the degree to which we remain steadfast regardless of what we see with our eyes. The degree to which we walk by faith is the degree to which we see our desired results manifest.

III.   Stick with the Word (Don't Give Up on the Word)

> Taking claim to God's promises is a vigorous discipline. Many of us give up in the first mile of the race when things don't look so good for the home team.
>
> —Connie D'Alessandro, from *The Spirit Is Calling*

Sometimes our results don't show up as quickly as we think they should. Sometimes it looks as if God forgets us or overlooks us as He blesses the person right beside us with the blessing we've been believing for! It doesn't help when we have well-meaning friends who mention all of the things they think we have done wrong and call them the reason the blessing has not shown up yet.

My instruction to you is to continue to exercise the principles listed in this section. If you are doing something wrong, God will let you know, and He will speak in a way that you will know He's the One

---

[122]   Webster.

[123]   See 2 Corinthians 5:7.

[124]   See Acts 20:24 KJV.

talking. Always be in the posture to receive from Him. Set yourself to be in agreement with Him—to the point that even when your mind does not yet comprehend, you receive truth because it bears witness with your spirit. God may choose to send someone to tell you where you've missed it, or you may hear Him in a sermon, a song, or any number of avenues. However God chooses to speak, you will recognize Him because the message will bear witness with your spirit.

When you hear Him, do not harden your heart.[125] Do not resist Him. Receive His correction and do what He says. If you choose not to do what He says, you will hinder Him from getting His blessings to you. You will have become your own hindrance.

As you continue to exercise these principles—regardless of how long it takes—*don't give up.* Stick to the Word. God's Word never returns without accomplishing what He sent it out to do.[126] Don't be weary in well-doing. You will reap if you don't faint.[127] Know that your labor (your faithfulness in God's Word) is not in vain.[128]

Isaiah 55:10–11
Galatians 6:9
1 Corinthians 15:58

---

[125] See Hebrews 3:15.

[126] See Isaiah 55:10–11.

[127] See Galatians 6:9.

[128] See 1 Corinthians 15:58.

IV.   Stay Full of the Word (Don't Contradict the Word)

During times of waiting, times of expecting, and times of testing, it is especially important to stay full of the Word. We should be full of the Word at all times, but especially during these times of waiting, expecting, and testing; it is during these times that it becomes very easy to get discouraged and to set the Word aside. But I hear Gloria Copeland say, "Don't give up. Double up!"[129] This is the time to double up on the Word!

I remember one night several years ago when I was taking a homiletics course at a Bible college. On this particular night, we did an in-class exercise in which the instructor told us to construct a sermon title around Luke 4:1: "And Jesus being full of the Holy Ghost returned from Jordan, and was led by the Spirit into the wilderness."

A title was brewing on the inside of me, but I could not discern the words to form the title as quickly as the instructor wanted me to. It was not until I got home after class that night that I heard the title as clear as day: *Be Careful What You Are Full Of, Because You Will Be Led By It.*

As we find ourselves between the "amen" of prayer and the manifestation of the promise, it is paramount that we stay full of God's Word. What we are full of is what we will be led by. If we are full of God's Word, we will be led by God's Word in our thoughts, in our actions, and, most importantly, in our words.

Why are our words so important? Because life and death are in the power of the tongue.[130] (God's Word is life.)[131] Whatever we speak is what we will get. If we speak life, we will get life. If we speak death, we

---

[129]   Gloria Copeland wrote a minibook entitled *Don't Give up—Double up*. Available for purchase at www.kcm.org.

[130]   See Proverbs 18:21.

[131]   See John 6:63.

will get death. We learn in James chapter 3 that though the tongue is a tiny member of the human body, it has tremendous power:

> A bit in the mouth of a horse controls the whole horse. A small rudder on a huge ship in the hands of a skilled captain sets a course in the face of the strongest winds. *A word out of your mouth may seem of no account, but it can accomplish nearly anything—or destroy it!* (James 3:3–5a MSG, emphasis added).

If we are full of doubt, we will be led by doubt. If we are full of unbelief, we will be led by unbelief. If we are full of negativity, we will be led by negativity. The person who says, "That'll never happen for me … nobody likes me … I'm sick … I'm broke," can expect just that: It will never happen for him. Nobody will like him. He will be sick. He will be broke.

On the other hand, if we are full of the faith, hope, and positivity that come from the Word, we will be led by the faith, hope, and positivity that come from the Word. The person who says, "If God can do it for them, I know He can do it for me," can expect that God will do it for him.[132] He who says, "I have favor with God and with man," can expect that people will show him favor.[133] The person who says, "By Jesus' stripes I am healed … my God supplies all my need according to His riches in glory," can expect healing to manifest in his body and provision to show up when he needs it.[134]

In a nutshell: you have what you say!

---

[132] See Hebrews 13:8.

[133] See Luke 2:52.

[134] See Isaiah 53:5; 1 Peter 2:24; Philippians 4:19.

Mark 11:23

Staying full of the Word will help us to speak positive words and to get positive results. Not just positive words, but God's words. Not just positive results, but God's results. If we are full of the Word, we will be led by the Word in speech, in action, in thought, and in intent. If we are full of the Word, we will speak the Word, for out of the abundance of the heart the mouth speaks.[135] However, if we are low on our supply of the Word and have allowed doubt, fear, unbelief, or any form of negativity to enter, we will become full of it and will speak that doubt, fear, unbelief, and negativity because, still, out of the abundance of the heart the mouth speaks.

> A good man brings good things out of the good stored up in his heart, and an evil man brings evil things out of the evil stored up in his heart. For the mouth speaks what the heart is full of (Luke 6:45 NIV).

We cannot afford to speak unbelief—not even a little bit. Even if we have spoken words of faith about a matter before, if we speak words of unbelief after having spoken words of faith, we cancel out those words of faith and reap the negative results.

---

[135] See Luke 6:45.

"But wait a minute!" you may say. *"I thought you said God's Word always does what God sent it out to do."*

I did. And it does. But remember – if you don't mix the Word with faith, it will not benefit you.[136] Neither will the Word benefit you if you mix faith with unbelief. Speaking words of faith, or even doing deeds of faith, with unbelief in your heart will hinder the desired results from manifesting. Such was the case with the disciples when they could not cast a demon out of a boy. When the disciples asked Jesus why they could not cast him out, Jesus told them it was because of their unbelief.[137]

Operating in faith and unbelief at the same time will cause you to be like a person who has no bearings—a person who has nothing to hold on to in order to steady himself. The Bible likens it to being tossed to and fro like a wave of the sea, and to being a double-minded man who is unstable in all his ways. A person who operates in a mixture of faith and unbelief should not expect to receive anything from the Lord.[138] Staying full of the Word will equip you with the boldness to ask of the Lord confidently in faith with nothing wavering, fully expecting to receive.

Overcoming Hindrances to Receiving

The last thing the devil wants is for you to believe God. He knows that if he can keep you from receiving God's Word, he can keep you from believing. Therefore, he does everything in his power to try to take God's Word from you. If he cannot take it from you, he will try to make you doubt it. If he cannot make you doubt it, he will try to make you abandon it.

In John 10:10, we learn that the thief, who is the devil, comes only to steal, to kill, and to destroy. He comes to steal the Word from our hearts to prevent it from taking root and to keep us from growing in God and

---

[136] See "Unbelievers vs. Disbelievers" on page xvi.

[137] See Matthew 17:19–29 KJV.

[138] See James 1:6–8.

seeing God's promises manifest in our lives.[139] If he is not able to steal the Word, he goes to plan B, which is to kill.

He attempts to kill the effect of the Word that we have received by bringing affliction and persecution to make us doubt the Word and thus keep it from taking effect in our lives.[140] Alas, if this tactic does not work, he goes to plan C, which is to destroy.

He attempts to destroy us by flooding us with the cares of this world—getting us to take our focus off God,[141] Who has already provided everything we need. He wants us to become our own gods by trying to provide for and take care of ourselves. He glamorizes riches, status, and other worldly things to divert our attention from pursuing God through His Word. If he can so divert our attention, getting us to neglect the Word as we pursue worldly lusts, he can choke the Word out of our lives.[142] However, if we continue to study the Word and meditate the Word in the midst of Satan's attempts to steal it and to distract us from it, we will bring forth fruit; we will see the results of what we have been believing for.[143]

I believe the primary way Satan sets out to accomplish his tasks of stealing, killing, and destroying is to plant fear in the hearts of believers. If he can get believers to fear that God is trying to hold something back from them, or that He will not do what He said He would do, he has an open door to draw them away from the Word or to steal the Word they have already received. Fear opens the door to doubt, which causes one to become double-minded, which in turn leads one to speak words that contradict the Word of God and thus to abort the manifestation of what he or she is believing for.

---

[139]   See Mark 4:15.

[140]   See Mark 4:17.

[141]   See Mark 4:19.

[142]   Ibid.

[143]   See Mark 4:20.

The way to overcome the fear that Satan would have us feel is to meditate on God's love, for perfect love casts out fear.[144] God has not given us the spirit of fear; He has given us the spirit of love.

> There is no fear in love; but perfect love casteth out fear: because fear hath torment … (1 John 4:18 KJV).

> For God has not given us a spirit of fear, but of power and of *love* and of a sound mind (2 Timothy 1:7 NKJV, emphasis added).

Anytime you feel tempted or pressured to feel fear, to doubt, or to waver regarding the Word of God, realize that the devil is a liar. Jesus said that Satan is a liar and the father of lies.[145] Jesus is the Way, the Truth, and the Life.[146] He came that we might have life—His very life—and that we might have it more abundantly.[147] He is not trying to keep anything from us. He is trying to get everything to us and has given us the formula for receiving it all:

> Seek the Kingdom of God above all else, and live righteously, and He will give you everything you need (Matthew 6:33 NLT).

Get these truths on the inside of you by meditating them.[148] Meditating God's Word is the key to overcoming the hindrances of fear, doubt, and double-mindedness that would cause us to speak contrary to God's Word, thus forfeiting the manifestation of God's promises. Meditate His Word constantly, always keeping His Word in your mouth (i.e., always speaking His Word).

---

[144]   See appendix A.

[145]   See John 8:44.

[146]   See John 14:6.

[147]   See John 10:10.

[148]   See "Meditate on the Word" on page 53

Meditating His Word will make His Word real to you. It will take root in you and will alleviate any room for fear and doubt to enter. Meditating His Word will cause you to be prosperous and to succeed. No matter how long it takes for the manifestation to appear, continue to meditate the Word, for you will bear fruit when it is time.

Conclusion

Thank you for joining me on this wonderful journey into the simple yet penetrating truth of God's Word. It is my prayer that you have been challenged to go deeper than you have ever gone into the things of God, that you have been encouraged in your walk, and that you received revelation needed for such a time as this.

May you continue to grow in the revelation of God's love for you, the understanding of God's heart to bless you, and the knowledge of all of the promises He has made available to you through His Son, Jesus Christ. May you walk more victoriously with each passing moment, enjoying the abundant life that Jesus came to give you.

Behold Him and you will be like Him, for what we behold is what we become.

If you received Jesus Christ as your Savior and Lord while reading this book, what a blessing it would be to hear from you! If you received the gift of the Holy Spirit with the evidence of speaking in tongues, or if you received your breakthrough or deliverance, let me hear from you! I want to celebrate God's goodness with you! E-mail your testimony to KatherineFreeMinistries@gmail.com.

***

Father,

I thank You for these precious ones. I thank You that seeds were planted and that seeds were watered. I bless You, Father, for giving the increase. Give them the spirit of wisdom and revelation in the knowledge of You. Enlighten the eyes of their understanding, that they may know the hope of Your calling and the riches of Your glory, and that they may know the immeasurable and unlimited and surpassing greatness of Your power in and for us who believe. Bind them to the revelations they have received and the victories they have won. I command thoughts of fear, doubt, and unbelief to loose them now, in the Name of Jesus. Seal them, Father, with Your precious Holy Spirit.

Thank You, Father, for Your *Sozo Package*. Thank You for blessing us with every spiritual blessing and with all things that pertain to life and godliness. Be Thou glorified as we behold Jesus and become more like Him. Be Thou magnified, Father, for You have pleasure in the prosperity of Your children!

Thank You, Lord! In Jesus' Name. Amen![149]

---

[149] This prayer is based on the following scriptures: 1 Corinthians 3:6; Ephesians 1:18–19; Matthew 18:18; Ephesians 1:13; Ephesians 1:3; 2 Peter 1:3; 1 John 3:2; Psalm 35:27.

Appendix A

Love Scriptures

Psalm 86:15 NLT

But you, O Lord, are a God of compassion and mercy, slow to get angry and filled with unfailing love and faithfulness.

Zephaniah 3:17 NIV

The LORD your God is with you, the Mighty Warrior who saves. He will take great delight in you; in His love He will no longer rebuke you, but will rejoice over you with singing."

John 3:16 KJV

For God so loved the world, that He gave his only begotten Son, that whosoever believeth in Him should not perish, but have everlasting life.

Romans 5:8 NIV

But God showed his great love for us by sending Christ to die for us while we were still sinners.

Romans 8:37–39 KJV

Nay, in all these things we are more than conquerors through Him that loved us.
For I am persuaded, that neither death, nor life, nor angels, nor principalities, nor powers, nor things present, nor things to come,

Nor height, nor depth, nor any other creature, shall be able to separate us from the love of God, which is in Christ Jesus our Lord.

Galatians 2:20 KJV

I am crucified with Christ: nevertheless I live; yet not I, but Christ liveth in me: and the life which I now live in the flesh I live by the faith of the Son of God, who loved me, and gave Himself for me.

Ephesians 2:4–5 Amplified, Classic Edition

God—so rich is He in His mercy! Because of and in order to satisfy the great and wonderful and intense love with which He loved us,

Even when we were dead (slain) by [our own] shortcomings and trespasses, He made us alive together in fellowship and in union with Christ; [He gave us the very life of Christ Himself, the same new life with which He quickened Him, for] it is by grace (His favor and mercy which you did not deserve) that you are saved (*delivered from judgment and made partakers of Christ's salvation*).

1 John 3:2 KJV

Behold, what manner of love the Father hath bestowed upon us, that we should be called the sons of God …

1 John 4:7–10 KJV

Beloved, let us love one another: for love is of God; and every one that loveth is born of God, and knoweth God.

He that loveth not knoweth not God; for God is love.

In this was manifested the love of God toward us, because that God sent His only begotten Son into the world, that we might live through Him.

Herein is love, not that we loved God, but that He loved us, and sent His Son to be the propitiation for our sins.

1 John 4:18 KJV

There is no fear in love; but perfect love casteth out fear: because fear hath torment. He that feareth is not made perfect in love.

Scripture Index

Forgiven Scriptures	Meditation/Word of God Scriptures	Answered Prayer Scriptures	Promise Scriptures	Prosperity Scriptures	Healing Scriptures	Protection Scriptures
Psalm 103:2–3	Joshua 1:8	Matthew 7:7–8	Romans 11:29	Deuteronomy 8:18	Exodus 15:26[150]	Psalm 46:1
Psalm 103:12	Job 23:12	Matthew 21:22	2 Corinthians 1:20	Deuteronomy 28:1–13[151]	Exodus 23:25	Isaiah 41:10
Isaiah 54:9	Psalm 1:1–3	Mark 11:23–24	Ephesians 1:3	Psalm 35:27	Psalm 91:9–10	Psalm 91:1–16
John 3:17	Psalm 119:105	John 14:13–14	James 1:17	Psalm 84:11	Psalm 103:1–5	Psalm 121:7–8
Romans 8:1	Psalm 119:140	John 15:7	2 Peter 1:3	Matthew 6:33	Psalm 107:20	Isaiah 54:17
2 Corinthians 5:17	Proverbs 4:20–23	James 1:5–8		Luke 12:32	Isaiah 53:4–5	2 Thessalonians 3:3
Hebrews 8:12	Jeremiah 15:16	1 John 5:14–15		3 John 2	Jeremiah 30:17	2 Timothy 4:18
	Matthew 4:4				Matthew 9:35	
	Romans 10:17				Matthew 15:30	
	1 Peter 1:25				Acts 10:30	
	2 Timothy 3:16				1 Peter 2:24	
	Hebrews 4:12					

[150] Jesus has already fulfilled all of the requirements for us to receive these blessings. We must only receive Jesus. When we receive Jesus, we receive His righteousness (His uprightness and right standing with God) and all of the blessings that His righteousness affords us.

[151] See footnote 150

Appendix C

Receiving the Baptism of the Holy Spirit

If you have received Jesus as your Savior and Lord and you want the power to live this new life that He has given you victoriously, I invite you to receive the baptism of the Holy Spirit. Receiving the baptism of the Holy Spirit is a different experience than receiving the indwelling of the Holy Spirit, which happens the moment you receive Jesus as Savior and Lord. However, receiving the baptism of the Holy Spirit is just as easy as receiving Jesus as your Savior and Lord. You may be asking, *"If I've received Jesus and the Holy Spirit already lives inside me, why do I need to receive the baptism of the Holy Spirit? What is the Holy Spirit?"*

What Is the Holy Spirit?

Holy Spirit is not a "what." He is a "Who." Holy Spirit (also referred to as Holy Ghost) is the third person in the Godhead; there is God the Father, God the Son, and God the Holy Spirit. God, though He is one Being, is triune; He functions as three different beings, so to speak. I, Katherine Free, am one being, yet I function as a teacher, a student, and an administrator. Though I operate in different functions, I am still one person. So it is with God. God is God, Jesus, and the Holy Spirit all at the same time.

My dear pastor, Dr. Walter L. Gibson, who has gone home to be with the Lord, enjoyed imparting this simple, yet profound message of the triune nature of God to his students and congregation: "God sends, Jesus saves, and Holy Ghost seals." To capture the essence of this message,

I wrote a poem to share at our Christmas celebration one year. It is called "My Favorite Thing."[152]

My Favorite Thing

God Sends

God sent His Son,
Who's the only One
To Which my soul could be won
And in the end, receive a "WELL DONE".

I was His before time had begun,
And there is none
Who can out-do

        re-do

           or un-do
That which God has done for me and you.

This is one of my favorite things!

Jesus Saves

Jesus entered my heart –
Which was only a start.
Said He'd never ever depart,
So we are never apart.

---

[152] The italicized portions of the poem are to be sung to the melody of the classic Christmas carol "My Favorite Things." I adapted the words but kept the melody. Sing it with me: "This is one of my favorite things!" I also included the melody of the contemporary remake "Just Remember" by one of my favorite worship artists, Fred Hammond. Again, I adapted the words but kept the melody. Sing with me: "I remember!" Try this one: "So I surrender! Surrender! Surrender!"

He came – His love, truth, and life to impart –
My soul to upstart
Where He'd reside

                inside

                    and abide
So I'd never have to fall apart.

This is one of my favorite things!

<u>Holy Ghost Seals</u>

Holy Ghost indwelled me.
Satan had to flee.
I was then free –
For God accepted me.

I had a new Family tree.
Salvation - a guarantee.
None could ever pluck,

                suck,

                    or abduct
This child He'd sealed for eternity.

This is one of my favorite things!

I Remember!

God sent His Son through a virgin birth.
Jesus saves people throughout the earth.
Holy Ghost seals us at rebirth.

I Remember!

God sent His Son one glorious day.

Jesus saves — He's the only Way.
Holy Ghost seals — in His care we stay.

So I Surrender!

Not my will, Lord, but Thine be done.
I can't be lukewarm — it's all or none.

I Surrender
My will and my way.

I Surrender
My life … I'll obey.

I Surrender
Day after day.

I Surrender!
      Surrender!
         Surrender!

It's not about me, and never has been.
It's about You — the perfect sacrifice for sin.

God, thank You for Your Son, Jesus Christ,
Whom You so lovingly sacrificed.
You had Your plan in place ALL THE WHILE
That me to You, You would reconcile.

Jesus — with all my heart I want to say,
"I bless You on this Christmas Day."
To my brothers and sisters in Christ,

Just remember:

Christmas is never to be about us.
For it was in eternity past when the Father said,
"Christ must."

And so He did.

THIS IS MY FAVORITE THING!

****

Indwelling of the Holy Spirit

When you receive Jesus as your Savior and Lord, the Holy Spirit comes to live inside of you to reproduce the very life of Jesus inside of you. So the life you now live is not yours. You have Jesus' life on the inside of you. The same sinless, holy life that Jesus walked out on this earth is the same life you have living on the inside of you—in your spirit.[153]

> Do you not know that you are the temple of God and that the Spirit of God dwells in you? (1 Corinthians 3:16 NKJV).

> And God has given us His Spirit as proof that we live in Him and He in us (1 John 4:13 NLT).

---

[153] Man is a three-part being consisting of spirit, soul, and body. See 2 Thessalonians 5:23. The spirit is the real us—the part that communes with God, and the only part of us God sees after we are born again. He sees us as being just as holy, pure, and anointed as Jesus because He sees us through the blood of Jesus. To gain better understanding of this truth, I recommend listening to Andrew Wommack's teaching *Spirit, Soul, and Body*, which is available for download and for purchase at Andrew Wommack Ministries International (www.awmi.net).

Because you are His sons, God sent the Spirit of His Son into our hearts, the Spirit who calls out, "Abba, Father" (Galatians 4:6 NIV).

I have been crucified with Christ. It is no longer I who live, but Christ who lives in me. And the life I now live in the flesh I live by faith in the Son of God, who loved me and gave Himself for me (Galatians 2:20 ESV).

It is through the indwelling of Holy Spirit that God develops godly character within us and molds us into the image of His dear Son, Jesus.

… And the Lord—who is the Spirit—makes us more and more like Him as we are changed into His glorious image (2 Corinthians 3:18 NLT).

Function of Holy Spirit

Holy Spirit comes to dwell inside of you the moment you receive Jesus as your Savior and Lord. He is on assignment from God the Father to teach us and to remind of all that Jesus has spoken and will ever speak to us. He is on assignment to correct us, to encourage us, to lead us, to comfort us, and to transform us into the image of Jesus and to seal us to God Himself. As the Spirit of Truth, Holy Spirit will speak only that which He has heard Jesus say. Jesus says only what He hears God say; therefore, Holy Spirit speaks only what God has said.[154]

But the Comforter (Counselor, Helper, Intercessor, Advocate, Strengthener, Standby), the Holy Spirit, Whom the Father will send in My Name [in my place, to represent Me and act on My behalf], He will teach you all things. And He will cause you to

---

[154] See John 7:16; 8:26, 28; 14:10.

recall (will remind you of, bring to your remembrance) everything
I have told you" (John 14:26 Amplified, Classic Edition).

"… When He, the Spirit of truth, has come, He will guide you
into all truth; for He will not speak on His own authority, but
whatever He hears He will speak; and He will tell you things to
come" (John 16:13 NKJV).

As you see in John 14:26, Holy Ghost serves many functions in
our lives. While it is beyond the scope of this book to go into depth about
the functions of the Holy Spirit, I would like to recommend that you read
Presenting the Holy Spirit by Sister Fuschia Pickett, who has gone home to
be with the Lord.[155] Outside of the Bible, this book is the most thorough
and comprehensive book I have seen where Holy Spirit is concerned. God
used this book as a foundational tool to introduce me to the Person of the
Holy Spirit years ago, and my life has not been the same since.

Relying on the Holy Spirit and allowing Him to operate fully in
each of His functions will empower you to live the victorious life that Jesus
came to give you. Receiving this life is one thing, but living it is another.
If we want to live victoriously—from glory to glory rather than from glory
to defeat to glory to defeat—we need the power of the Holy Ghost.

Baptism of the Holy Spirit

Before returning to Heaven, Jesus told His disciples that they would receive
power after the Holy Spirit came upon them (i.e., after they were baptized
in the Holy Spirit).

---

[155] Fuschia Pickett, *Presenting the Holy Spirit* (Lake Mary, Florida: Charisma House, 1997).

> But you will receive power when the Holy Spirit comes on you;
> and you will be my witnesses in Jerusalem, and in all Judea and
> Samaria, and to the ends of the earth" (Acts 1:8 NIV).

The word "power" in the preceding scripture comes from the Greek word "*dunamis,*" which is where we get the English word "dynamite."[156] The word "*dunamis*" means "ability, abundance, might, power, and strength."[157] Jesus explained to the disciples that when they received the baptism of the Holy Spirit, they would receive the power of the Holy Spirit, which would enable them to be His witnesses—to boldly tell others what they had witnessed during His time on the earth, and to tell it in a way that others would understand. They witnessed the miracles that He performed. They witnessed the love He shared and the compassion He showed. They witnessed His death. They witnessed His burial. They witnessed His resurrection. And now they had the boldness to tell everyone about it. On the day of Pentecost, when they received the baptism of the Holy Spirit, they received the power to speak to every man in his own language through the utterance of other tongues (languages).[158]

When we receive the baptism of the Holy Spirit, we receive the same power, the same boldness, and the same utterance. We receive the empowerment to tell of all that God has done in our lives and to be His show-and-tell as we live out the promises that He has given us. As His witnesses, we receive the empowerment to hold on to God's promises, to live above sin, and to overcome even during the vicissitudes of life.

This empowerment is made available to every born-again believer. It is part of our *Sozo Package.* God has made this empowerment available through the baptism of His precious Holy Spirit to all who would choose to receive it. It is only a matter of asking:

---

156   *Strong's Greek*, word 1411.

157   Ibid.

158   See Acts 2:1–11.

For everyone who asks receives; the one who seeks finds; and to
the one who knocks, the door will be opened.

Which of you fathers, if your son asks for a fish, will give him a
snake instead?

Or if he asks for an egg, will give him a scorpion? If you then,
though you are evil, know how to give good gifts to your children,
how much more will your Father in heaven give the Holy Spirit to those
who ask Him!" (Luke 11:10–13 NIV, emphasis added).

Praying in the Holy Spirit

The baptism of the Holy Spirit comes with a new prayer language—a
heavenly language that allows you to communicate directly with God,
spirit to Spirit,[159] thereby building yourself up in faith and keeping yourself
mindful of the love of God. This heavenly language is referred to as
speaking in unknown tongues or praying in the Spirit / Holy Ghost.

> For one who speaks in a tongue speaks not to men but to God;
> for no one understands him, but he utters mysteries in the Spirit
> (1 Corinthians 14:2 ESV).

> But ye, beloved, building up yourselves on your most holy faith,
> praying in the Holy Ghost,
> Keep yourselves in the love of God … (Jude 20, 21 KJV).

Some people think that tongues and the baptism of the Holy Ghost
were just for those in biblical times. Other people think that speaking in
tongues is of the devil. However, we who receive the Word of God as truth
believe and know that the baptism of the Holy Ghost with the evidence of
speaking in tongues is a gift of God. We believe and know that it is just as
real and as relevant today as it was in biblical times. For those of you who

---

[159] See John 4:24.

don't know, choose to believe the Word of God is truth and choose to receive all that God has for you. God will manifest Himself and the truth of His Word to you in a very personal way so you know you have heard from Him.

If you are a believer and you would like to receive the baptism of the Holy Spirit with the evidence of speaking in tongues, you can receive it right now. Whether you've been saved for years, days, or even moments does not matter. Your time is now. Simply pray this prayer and receive:

Father,

Thank You so much for your love. Thank You for giving me Jesus. Thank You for being the Giver of every good and every perfect gift. Thank You for the gift of the Holy Spirit. I ask you to fill me with the Holy Spirit. I receive the baptism of the Holy Spirit now. I receive Your supernatural power, Your supernatural abundance, Your supernatural strength, Your supernatural might, and Your supernatural ability to be a witness for You. I receive my prayer language. I receive my praise language. I thank You for it now, in Jesus' Name. Amen.

Hallelujah!

*I celebrate with you as you plumb to deeper depths
and soar to higher heights in God by His Spirit!*

Now take your praise language by faith. Open your mouth and begin to speak. Don't try to make sense of it. Speak the words and the syllables that you hear on the inside. My friend once told me of her husband's experience the first time he spoke in unknown tongues. She had not spoken in unknown tongues at that time and asked him what it was like. He said, "There were a lot of *A*s and a lot of *L*s." That description sounds funny (and we had a good Holy Ghost–inspired laugh over it), but his description was a very accurate portrayal of what he heard in his spirit and what he spoke out loud. Don't try to make sense of it. Just speak what you hear. Holy Spirit will give you the words, but He will not take control of your mouth. *You* need to do the speaking.

Go ahead.…

Begin to speak ….

***

Thank You, Father, for these who have received. I speak that the seeds that have been planted have taken root in good soil, that they cannot be plucked up. I thank You that my brothers and sisters bring forth fruit that remains— one hundredfold. I thank You for new levels of victory in their lives. I thank You for taking them to deeper levels of revelation in You. I thank You, Lord, that out of their bellies flow rivers of living water. I thank You for equipping them for the work that You have for them to do, and for giving them the utterance and the boldness to be witnesses for you. I thank You for sealing them with Your precious Holy Spirit, in Jesus' Name. Amen.[160]

If you received the baptism of the Holy Spirit with the evidence of speaking in tongues, let me hear from you! I want to celebrate the goodness of God with you! E-mail your testimony to KatherineFreeMinistries@ gmail.com. God bless you!

May you continue in the things that you have learned and have been assured of, knowing of Whom you have learned them (2 Timothy 3:14), in Jesus' Name.

Love,
Katherine

---

[160] This prayer is based on the following scriptures: Mark 4:20, John 7:38, 2 Timothy 3:17, Ephesians 6:19, Acts 1:8, Ephesians 1:13.

Printed in the United States
By Bookmasters